"Breaking Reality"

and

Other Explorations in Consciousness

Transcription of Selected Talks by
Tilak

Edited by Dr. Elizabeth B. Buck

EBB PUBLISHING

Las Vegas
Colorado Springs

"Breaking Reality" and Other Explorations in Consciousness

©2000 Tilak S. Fernando

ISBN 0-9631529-4-7

Library of Congress Card Number: 00-109219

EBB Publishing
675 Blackhawk Drive
Colorado Springs, Colorado 80919
USA

This book is dedicated to Janaka, Aneya and Orion.

Acknowledgments

This book is the result of dedication and love on the part of numerous individuals. With special gratitude to Jane Hart for creative design of the book; Betsy Buck for initiating this project, editing and inspirational support; Lisa Gizara for her exceptional photography; and Mindy Krasner, Tom Umholtz and Lee Stein for their invaluable assistance. Also my special thanks to Ron Faithful, Jim Gair, Aveline Hoffman and Alan Weinberger for their contributions in helping make this book possible.

Preface

This book is not about your life. It is not even about your mind. Rather it is about the way your mind takes you on a trip. Within these pages, you will survey, map, scale and display your trip. As a result, you'll know the routes for scenic trips and the places to avoid or that require extra caution. You will have a practical guide, showing you how to have fun. Period. It does not focus on the misery of the many mind *attacks* that happen in everyday life, which, unfortunately, most people accept as normal or commonplace.

Comprised of a series of talks by Tilak, which have been transcribed and minimally edited for the enjoyment and enrichment of the reader, this volume of selected essays is for people who want to express what they feel without fear of being harassed by their own minds. It is also not about deep concepts of psychopathology, psychodynamics, or a method to produce deep insights into your psyche nor about neurosis, psychotherapy, or personal development. However, you will be shown, in a simple and common-sense way, how your mind jerks you around and more importantly, how to transform this cycle into an ongoing experience of great joy and pleasure.

Like the darkness before a storm or the lightning and thunder before a hurricane, your mind sends you signals before an *attack*. Based on the material in these pages, you will be able to identify these signals and take quick, appropriate actions. These actions will alter the direction of your mind's intent to either punish or belittle who you really are. What will be revealed are the many different maps drawn by your mind that target you, in the short term, for maximum assault throughout your day and night. You will learn that your mind also generates long-range plans designed to sabotage your joy of living. This book is for everyday, ordinary people, neurotic or not, who are dealing with day-to-day life situations, bombarded by problems, crazy situations or undeniable limitations, offering a way to turn any life situation into a fun-filled space.

Finally, Tilak's words here lead into the path of liberation. Great teachers of all ages have talked about achieving liberation. Some traditions claim that liberation requires many lifetimes. Others says that it is in a moment. The reader will have the joy of seeing sense and nonsense, the myths and realities about freedom and liberation in the way the nine wheels of liberation are introduced to you. To see many fantasies and tricks of the mind and not get carried away by them can be a source of pleasure. Like a truly fine sword, the nine wheels of liberation cut through your mind's schemes and attacks and take you to a space of freshness and joy.

As Tilak says, his talks are not about educating or repairing somebody for a better life. These are spontaneous talks -- just like love poems-- given to a group of people out of pure appreciation. The effect of these talks is to awaken us from the way we have put ourselves into trance-like states by our stories. Reading these words, we hope they may ignite your passion, to give you a jump-start with a point of brilliance -- or you may be carried away from a serious holding pattern into waves of light, to realize nothing is a big deal.

Jane Hart, Los Angeles, September 2000

To Bobby Allan

[signature]

10-27-01

"Breaking Reality"
and
Other Explorations in Consciousness

Table of Contents

"Breaking Reality"
and
Other Explorations in Consciousness

"Breaking Reality" and Other Explorations in Consciousness

The speed of light is higher than the speed of sound.

The speed of thought is higher than the speed of light.

Break the speed of thought, and you will break time.

"Breaking Reality" and Other Explorations in Consciousness

Breaking Reality

Life is an invitation. Life is an adventure. It is a challenge to liberate from our limitations and capacities as human beings to something that is not obvious to us. You don't understand life. You can't understand life. What you know is what appears to you as real: the world, the things you can see -- whatever appears to you. That is what can be called your reality. In this life all the pleasures and the joys that we can think of are coming out of either improving or adding to something that already exists as a source of pleasure, or getting rid of something that we feel is unwanted by us. But breaking this reality is to experience a pleasure or a joy that we have not touched before, or to experience an emotion or energy that we have not tasted in our life.

You all think about life. But when you think about awakening, or freedom, or enlightenment, or personal development, you are creating a point of arrival in your story. They're all actually geared toward the one thing you believe is real -- what you call "reality." So when you attempt to speak about life, you are not really speaking about life; you are speaking only about your contact with a reality in which you're trying to make sense. Since you are limited to considering only things that relate to your contact with reality, you are unable to see anything but the most obvious reasons for your interactions and changes of direction. Yet behind these reasons, and hidden behind the appearance of reality, are many entrances to the mystery of life.

For example, why do you go to a restaurant? To eat? Why do you go to a party? You go to a restaurant not because you are hungry. That is an excuse to go. You can eat at home; if you're hungry you can make some food. You don't go to a restaurant in order to eat. You go to a restaurant in order to have fun. You go to a restaurant to eat in order to have fun. Only very few people come all alone to eat in a restaurant. In a way they are pathetic cases; you even feel sorry for those who are eating all alone. Very rarely do you go to a restaurant alone to eat. You go to a restaurant to have fun. What is fun? Experiencing the pleasure of being together. That is what's called fun. Fun is actually exposing and experiencing the pleasure of being together.

So what does this have to do with life? Everything. This is exactly the beat of life. You are born. You arrive. You arrive to a party because you are invited. You are not invited to a party to have a bad time. In the same way, you come here into life to have fun -- to experience the pleasure of being together. You are not just here because you are hungry. You are not merely greedy for food. However, your hunger and greediness are the excuses which make it possible for someone to throw the party so that you may arrive! It is a way to bring your presence into existence. You become alive and real. Then the simple pleasure of being together with others becomes the way life is allowed to unfold as love. So the lust is the desire that makes you really get out from you, and go into another place. The force of attraction. Without feeling that arousal, you wouldn't move from yourself. You need that in order to move.

The most natural thing about reality is your hunger. You are hungry. The most natural thing about life, the most sacred thing about the opening of life, is hunger. It is your craving. So the most natural opening of life is actually hunger. That is how you are here and that is why you are yearning. But that hunger, the food, is only a call. This is how it is set up for you to come to a restaurant. Hunger doesn't mean that you eat and then go to sleep. It is actually a point for you to see some direction -- to see where the fun is at. Fun is not in the food. Fun is really in the party itself, which invites you, makes you crazy to eat, puts you out of your house, and moves you into a place where a gathering can occur. This hunger, and your movement to fulfill it, lead you to inquire about what it is that you are made of.

What you are made of is lust. Lust. You are a living furnace. Like anything in this carbon cycle existence, you have a birth, life span and death. Everything from the smallest particle or insect you can see to the furthermost stars and largest galaxies in the universe: they are born, they ignite, and they die. Everything in this reality is engaged in this process of appearance and disappearance. So your hunger, your craving, is the natural core of your existence. Fire. It makes it possible for you to bring yourself into a state of "body heat." The craving -- the arousal -- is the hunger that brings you to the restaurant we call "the zone of wonder." The foods that are served there all contain one ingredient called "fascination." The pleasure of sharing this food, and of being in a state of attraction, brings your life into a "charged field." Then you are Awake and Alive! But the presence of hunger and lust also subtly indicates something else. You are always either in a state of attraction (wonder) or a state of worry about getting fed. However invisible it may seem to you, you are always leaning towards something.

What does "leaning towards" mean? It means you are never in balance. There is nothing that is ever in balance. This is called the imperfection. This imperfection -- this lack of balance -- is what causes the motion. There is nothing in balance; at every moment your life is leaning. You are always leaning towards something. You may be leaning towards joy, leaning towards fear, leaning towards excitement, leaning towards death, or even leaning towards becoming alive. There is no way for you to be in equilibrium or in balance.

There is not even anything called balance. There is no

point where everything is just in order. If everything were so in order, what would happen? It would be dead; there would be no motion. There is no such thing. But it is fascinating the way you have attempted to create that. You created the notion of "harmony" as a way to relate to what you call imperfection. Imperfection, in fact, is the beauty. Without imperfection there is no beauty. The beauty of a dance, like the beauty of life, is that everything is in a process of leaning towards something. Leaning towards. Not attached, remember, leaning. Leaning means that you don't give weight. Attraction is more like a force; leaning means you are leaning towards somebody or something. That's also very different than moving. Moving is not leaning. Leaning means, for example, that you are leaning towards sleep, or you are leaning towards waking up. But you have a lot of trouble with leaning. You have a lot of trouble with imperfection. You can't see how everything is really just perfectly imperfect. If anything were perfectly perfect there would be no existence. It would collapse. The only perfect body is a dead body. It has no leanings, and it has no motion. If even just one point in space were perfectly perfect, there would be nothing there. No person can be perfectly perfect, and there is a certain beauty in that. Humility and innocence are its faces. When you are uneasy, it is because you are trying to make sense with your imperfection. You are trying to find reasons for your imperfection. You are trying to find a purpose for life. You are trying to find a meaning in life. You are trying to achieve goals. This immediately creates boundaries, which immediately creates a form, which immediately creates "reality." And when you are in this reality -- the reality which you have created out of the imperfection -- it wraps you with what is called time, and puts you into a cocoon. The friction you experience against time creates the wear and tear. Therefore you have the suffering. Therefore you have the pain.

Do you know the deepest joy you can have? It is this.

What does "this" mean? This. The deepest joy is this. When I say "this," there is nothing in it. When I say nothing, I do not mean a void or an emptiness. It has no references; it has no point; it has no time. There is no such thing called "this moment." Remember, there is no such thing called "this moment." There is only this space. This space. This space is an opening. An opening. The deepest joy in life is actually this. If you say it in one word, it's "this." "This" means an opening, nothing else. What does an opening bring? Something suddenly becomes clear. In life, the most natural forces that come are openings. What you do in life is close them. But when an opening has occurred, through that opening comes a passage, a window, or a gateway of no effort -- no energy. Opening brings a new beginning, a freshness, beauty and clarity without your effort.

But you always try to close the openings. All the time what you do is try to find extremely pleasurable ways of going to sleep. After you have so much sex and food and pleasure and everything, what you think about is going to bed -- getting to your pillow. You are really just trying to get super exhausted. What you are really trying to get in life is super-exhausted. Nothing else. So you engage in super-stimulation, sex, power, energy, and achievement in order to find what? It looks like all the pleasures and building of energy finally come to a point of climax and explodes. Then what happens? Then the point of maximum exhaustion in which you collapse seems the most pleasurable point of arrival. To have the most pleasurable sleep. You are trying to get into the most pleasurable sleep that is possible in life. All the activities you are doing are geared finally for you to go down and disappear -- to have the most deeply pleasurable sleep. In order to create the pleasurable sleep you have to create so much energy and effort. Closure. Contact. But the opening is natural. Opening has no energy. Like the Kuwaiti oil wells. They are naturally coming out. The oil comes to the surface with the most natural unbelievable force. Now you can't even close the burning wells.   They are so difficult to close.   You don't need to search for openings.   Openings are there -- you just discover them, like oil wells.   You discover the openings -- that's all.   And they are there.

An opening is just a point of realization.   Just like the oil wells, they are here.   The openings are with you.   But unlike the oil wells, the openings are invisible.   They are odorless, they are colorless, and they are untouchable.   You can't just see them. You can't find the openings.   You are looking for something that has as odor.   You are looking for something that is related to your five senses.   The most important thing to realize is that the opening is always there.   An opening is what in you?   It's the spontaneous flow of life energy.   What is opening in you is nothing else but the spontaneous flow of life force that is going through you day and night. And also opening means a gateway of new ventilation and light coming into your existence.   An opening is seen spontaneously without memory and knowledge, and puts you into a highly charged field of energy.

So, truly speaking, the imperfection means nothing but spontaneity.   Not just spontaneity, but total spontaneity.   That is why it is called perfectly imperfect.   Right now, your spontaneity is imperfectly imperfect because it is not really spontaneous.   You like to be outrageous.   You like to be rebellious, but a little bit only.   It doesn't come out as a full, natural force.   In fact, the times you thought you were spontaneous, you probably were only impulsive -- not naturally breaking out.   Impulse is not spontaneity.   Most of the time, you explode.   You explode out of tension, out of building up in a closed frame.   It becomes destructive. Spontaneity is not an explosion but a natural overflow.   It is an overflow that becomes possible as an opening.   The entrance has never been closed.

So when I say you cut your spontaneity, what it means is that you have stopped the natural overflow of the life force. How do you do that? By fear. Fear of what? What do you really fear? You fear time. You fear time. What time do you fear? Your past? Your present? No, there is only one fear you have: your fear of the future. You're frightened of the next second. You have nothing to fear in the past; you cannot have. What you really fear is the future. You cannot have a fear of the past. What you fear is what will happen, what will come, and what will occur. You're frightened of it, and that's why your spontaneity is cut. Your spontaneity is cut by your fear of time, which is really a sense of the future. You don't have a past, even though you feel that your spontaneity is being cut by guilt, pain and shame. Those are just traps that are coming through your unworthiness. There are no such things as guilt or shame.

In order for you to punish yourself, the unworthiness creates a space called future. You'll be punished when? In the future. Can you be punished in the past? No, so you don't have to worry about the past. You are punished in the future. All these things are nothing but what? Thoughts. But what are thoughts? What you are worried about are the repercussions of the past manifesting in the future. Whatever you may call it -- guilt, karma, cause and effect, or other things -- it exists only in your mind. But your mind only exists now. Your mind has no past, your mind has no future, your mind has no present. Your mind has only this space, right now. It never had a past. The past is only an echo coming through the unworthiness in order to punish you. What you are engaged in is actually a process of punishment -- a sort of suicide which comes in a very fascinating way.

The future exists as a space for you to get your punishment for what you did in the past. Why do you do this? Because you are trapped within the imperfection. When it is not in total spontaneity, the imperfection immediately creates the boundary.

By creating a boundary, you have created a form. An order. A harmony. You immediately think in terms of harmony, perfection, and balance. When you have done something bad, you think you should have an equal amount of punishment. You've done this, so you should be given that. You have done left, so you should be given right. You have done white, so you should be given black. You think there is a thing called balance. You think there is a thing called order. You think there is a thing called harmony. You think there is a thing called perfection. And you are trapped in this belief. Do you get it? You are trapped in it. You are trapped in an illusion called order. You are trapped in an illusion called perfection. You are trapped in a thing called time, which doesn't exist.

This is an important thing to understand. Don't try to worry about how you will not suffer and what will happen. If you understand the nature of your traps, they will immediately evaporate. Because the traps are not made out of solid realities. Traps are made of illusory boundaries. You can cut through these illusory boundaries with the sword of wisdom. Cutting with the sword of wisdom means cutting through the boundary. Boundaries are limitations -- the known realities. The knowledge and information. All the things you have. Cutting through the boundary means the disappearance of the known. You are troubled by what is known to you -- nothing else. What is troubling you is what is known to you. Remember that. What is known to you as your life or your past is your trouble.

Cutting through the boundary of knowledge or information -- all the heaviness you are having -- cutting through the boundary means the disappearance of the known, and the appearance of intelligence. The intelligence is not information. All the information and knowledge you have are geared for one thing: survival. What you have not seen are the laws, the order of nature, that remain without any purpose of survival. What you see always has a goal, a purpose, a meaning -- a reference point to reality or to your body. What you have seen is the total picture of the beauty itself. You only engage in day-to-day life the way it looks to you on the surface. You are concerned with mundane survival, personal relations, success, making money. They're all actually about nothing else but survival -- maintaining your life. And you believe somehow or other that if you maintain it to the highest degree, you will be very happy and excited: "This is life." Your effort and energy are geared for survival, you understand. You can't break it. You think, "This is it. I mean, what else is there? I can't think. Maybe God, maybe life. Maybe I'm dead, there's no other life." But that's all about survival.

If you are truly in touch with the life force, all of those things that you normally think about -- they begin to happen without your effort. All the things that are there naturally come together without your effort. So if you really ask, "What is life about?" you may call it an adventure. It is about finding out and coming into understanding and then breaking that understanding so that the understanding disappears. In order to release the understanding, you have to have understanding. You have to have a way to surrender. When you say you have to drop something, you first have to have something to drop.

People come and say, "Oh, I'd like to come and give my things to you." No you don't. You'd like to give the things you don't want to have. You will never give things you hold precious and valuable. You want to give things you don't want to have. "Hey, Tilak, you want some books? Some precious articles, tables maybe?" No. What is precious to you is what you think is need-ed for your survival. What is precious to you is what is needed for your survival. What you are worried about is that your means of survival will be taken away. Then you will die. You will disap-pear. You will be in pain. You will suffer. But it is actually very different. It is much different. Much different. In fact, the

9

whole imperfection is about survival.

Complete spontaneity is not survival. Complete spontaneity is breaking out from the survival. It is the deepest breaking out from time. That is so beautiful to understand. Understanding this is different from knowledge. It is wisdom. What is wisdom? Wisdom is when you stop justifying, rationalizing, and giving excuses. Intelligence means spontaneous adaptation. Spontaneous adaptation to motion, sound, and light. Like the navigator of a boat, you have to know how to respond instantly as the changes come. You have no trouble then. You're perfectly imperfect so that whatever comes, you flow with it. You are still smooth. When you are not perfectly imperfect you try to use things. You try to use knowledge, principles, and manipulations. You try to manipulate in order to get it.

Spontaneous adaptation means meeting the passion and the compassion at the same speed. You have two different speeds for your passion and your forms of love or compassion. They're separate in you, like the body and mind you normally think of. Spontaneous adaptation means there's a dance. What is the dance, then? Leaning. Leaning for what? Whatever that is taking place. But in your case, whenever you are leaning, you also create friction because you try to pull yourself away from whatever you are leaning towards. This creates resistance. You create resistance when you pull yourself away from whatever you consider to be bad stuff. That's why I say the best joy you have is judgment. Good or bad. It happens in you immediately. The best joy you have in life is judgment. That's why you believe in order. There's judgment in it. In the true harmony of life, you keep in motion with whatever it is that comes along. That's the beauty.

You are also out of spontaneity for another reason. It is because you have enjoyed the space of fusion. The space of fusion is when you are fused together -- when you are glued together. You like to glue yourself together with something because you have learned to know your presence by being pressed against something else. You have not learned to know your presence in space alone. In space alone you panic. Space alone you experience as loneliness. Space alone you experience as separation. Space alone you experience as a dullness. Space alone you experience as a void. Space alone you experience as death. This is because of your ignorance about fusion. And what is fusion? What is attachment? Attachment is the way you see life. The way you see reality. The way you see the boundary.

Your attachment is really with one thing: it is with time. You are not living for now. You are living for tomorrow. That's your fusion. You are fused with time, nothing else. You are fused only with time. Your joy in life comes with the fusion of time. That creates fantasies, wishful thinking, daydreams, hope. That keeps you moving one way or the other. The only way to "un-fuse" is to kill it. What can you kill? What can you destroy? You can kill death. What you can kill is the death in you. Within yourself, remember, it is not your organs that are tense and give illnesses. In yourself you are slowly contracting. Contracting. That is why you are in a panic to expand and touch everything. You are in a slow contraction. That's why you are in a hurry to touch everything. It's like a shadow. There is a sense of shadow inside you -- a place where the light has not reached. And the shadow is slowly pulsating and trying to do what? Extend its arms to other places. The shadow of death. The shadow of darkness. Darkness is ignorance. Shadow, in the deepest sense, is ignorance. But ignorance is not "not knowing." It's more than not knowing. It's a space. Like a black hole in outer space, with a full gravitational force.

What you can kill is the death in you. When you can kill the death in you, what are you really killing? How do you die? You die through time. That's the end of time. What you are truly killing, in an organic sense, is your attachment with time. You can't just kill time, as such. What you can do is disconnect. When you can really disconnect from what is called time within you, it immediately puts you into a state, a space, which has no purpose. It puts you into a space which has no purpose, no intention, no direction. As long as you have a direction in which you are trying to move you are leaning towards the future.

But if you are in a space without anything, you are in a space with a full presence of everything that is there. If you are in a space with a full presence of everything, it's not that you will not function tomorrow. All the functions come, in complete detail. Your functions are not in detail yet. Everything comes into total detail. Everything makes sense. You are with everything. That's when you realize you are in a restaurant, having great fun in the pleasure of simply being together. With everyone. With everything. The food is still on the table --

"Breaking Reality" and Other Explorations in Consciousness

"Breaking Reality" and Other Explorations in Consciousness

Your visions are hopes, fantasies and wishful thinking.
Inner Visions is a kaleidoscope of the ever-changing beauty of
reality.

"Breaking Reality" and Other Explorations in Consciousness

Inner Visions

Inner Visions is a simple exploration into consciousness and reality. It is a way of understanding the challenges which are thrown into your life, as well as a way of discovering the beauty, excitement and exhilaration that life can offer. As a human being, your primary condition of being is consciousness, that which creates thinking and thoughts. Without consciousness you would never be able to experience totally the richness, joy and beauty that come to you in your lifetime.

Your experiences are one of two kinds. There are experiences of the senses through which you receive various stimuli and input. There are also experiences which come in a deeply subtle way from your connection with life through consciousness, or thinking and thoughts. Sensual experiences are your outer visions. It is through your thinking and thoughts that you create both the life you live and the world in which you live it. Through your five senses you experience what you feel when you create. Thus, it is very important to take a good, close look at what you create within your lifetime.

Life offers you every possibility to explore and to play, to receive the greatest nourishment and the greatest joy imaginable. Why then do you so often find that you have all types of blocks, hurdles and problems which interfere with having fun and playing with life? If you take a good look at where you are and what is happening with your life at any given moment, you can probably identify three major forces which hinder your harmonious connection with life. The three major forces are attacks, distractions and distortions. They happen in your consciousness. Since the primary condition of being is consciousness, whatever happens in your consciousness is vital to you. If something happens in your consciousness that takes you away from the natural flow of life within you, it becomes extremely important to return to a state of balance in order to continue your natural flow with life.

An attack can be described as a sudden impact into your awareness; it happens at a time of complete vulnerability which results when an unexpected circumstance of unknown origin occurs. Perhaps someone calls with bad news, or you plan something and things do not work out the way you want. You get off balance in a brief moment. On top of that something else does not go the way you expected and you become even further off balance. Anything that catches you by surprise and at the same time takes your awareness, stability and energy can be called an attack. An attack gives the appearance of occurring from a distance, from outside of you. It gives you the illusion that it is an external attack into your being where you become the victim rather than the creator.

However, if you examine it closely, an attack never occurs without your full participation. No attack can ever happen unless you participate in the event. You are not the poor helpless victim of some great external force which causes things to happen without your control or without any connection to you. Although you mayfeel that you are a helpless victim to your attacks, nevertheless, with or without your knowledge, you take an active role in every attack into your consciousness. You are not completely stable during an attack. In fact, most of the time you are not in complete stability at all, even though stability is not very difficult to achieve. The more you try to be stable, the more it will elude you. It is very rare to have a full day in which you are very aware and very relaxed at the same time.

If you examine where you are most of the time, you will find that you are preoccupied with some thought or attachment which you are either trying to release or trying to maintain. Usually you are in a battle to lose or to hold a thought, feeling, or memory of something someone said or did to you. You are in a grip, a confinement. You are not free and flexible most of the time so that when a sudden impact comes into your consciousness you are unable to adapt to the situation. Often because of your conflicts or your constrictions your awareness can be changed totally without your conscious knowledge. When an attack occurs, your lack of awareness evokes an immediate panic response in your consciousness.

Your whole system goes into panic the moment an attack happens. The panic then usually results in judgments and you end up telling yourself that "something very bad is going to happen, something worse is happening, I am finished, I am helpless, I am worthless." Whatever the words you choose to use, you set a chain reaction into motion. It is interesting to observe the overall process of what happens to you when an attack into your consciousness occurs.

First, you were not totally alert. You were merely drifting here and there with a thought or sensation and lost your alertness. Suddenly, something triggers, which seems to attack you from the outside, entering into your awareness. Next, panic strikes. With the panic, the energy form of the whole system changes. Your structure changes. Your mood changes. You become depressed, sad or angry. Everything seems to be rushing in your body. Then comes the emotional reaction. Your feelings and judgments arise, carrying with them a sense that something is bad, and that you are worthless. All of your senses seem to confirm this.   This is what triggers your feelings of helplessness.

Obviously, this is an area in which you must be extremely careful.   Once this chain of events is triggered by an attack into the consciousness, you have a tendency to rush and do things you later regret.   Most of the things you do in a situation like this, you do because your alertness has been distorted.   Since an attack can happen only in your three-dimensional thought patterns -- time, space, and patience -- you must cultivate your patience (or the art of waiting) in order to handle an attack.   Waiting has to come naturally.   If you are able to develop your patience, you will then be able to go into silence if an attack is triggered.   It is patience alone which permits the attack to pass away without a chain reaction occurring.   Since the very nature of reality is change, everything is subject to change.   Even an attack cannot last forever. Whatever happens in your consciousness happens as a way of changing one thing to another.   Usually, because of your panic mechanism, you will find that you allow yourself to be led by the panic into other areas which can trigger more attacks.

Additional distractions and distortions may then join hands making you feel totally helpless in a situation that has occurred due to your lack of awareness.   Attack is an essential phenomenon to study because it can happen to anyone at any time.   It is not something from the periphery, rather, it is a sudden impact into your consciousness.   Rather than reacting in a way that triggers a chain reaction, you need to learn to observe it and wait until it passes away.   You can gain strength and develop an ability to see clearly the challenges in any life situation.   When you judge something negatively in any way, you do not see the actual significance of what is happening.   There is nothing insignificant in life.   Every moment, every single thing that happens has a pattern, a significance, a meaning and a reality of its own.   Ordinarily you are not able to see it because you lose your reality in the confusion you create.

The second important force in consciousness is distraction. Distraction, although most easily understood, may be the most difficult hurdle. For example, you may want to concentrate on some important work and a mosquito may come and disturb you. Although it may look like the mosquito is the reason for your inability to concentrate, most of the time you will find that you have created the situation. Knowingly or unknowingly, you may have created enough room for a distraction to occur. Without your conscious knowledge, you may have slowly drifted into areas of fantasy and memory or you may be having a conversation with yourself, an internal dialogue. You find that you have completely lost the reality of what you are doing or saying.

A distraction may even come in a disguised way as absent-mindedness or forgetfulness. It may drain your energy when you allow yourself to drift into the areas of memory and fantasy which make you lose the vital forms that are available for your functioning in the moment. There may actually be moments when you find that you want the strength and the ability to think and it is not available to you. If you stop to look, even now, at this moment, you may be engaged in various activities and not focused on a sole channel. Your energy then becomes diverted and your consciousness is not truly steady and calm. You lack focus. For your normal functioning you should strive to be like a hollow bamboo reed where the air flows through unimpaired. When this occurs, your energy will flow in a streamlined manner into a singular focus where you are really moving with whatever is happening in the moment. This enables you to have more fun and play with life.

Distraction can be viewed as a force which comes and takes the vitality out of your existence. Unlike an attack into your consciousness, you can usually see a distraction coming. Like a storm or a tornado, you can see it on the horizon. As with an attack, a distraction causes you to feel helpless and nearly paralyzed. You are unable to get out of the way or to remove the distraction coming towards you. It can be very subtle. A distraction can even give you a sense of exhilaration in order to get your attention into something unknown. You may be carried away into an exciting, stimulating memory or a fantasy of wishful thoughts and dreams about the future. These may give you a temporary sense of exhilaration. However, the moment the thought is finished or the act is over you are left with a greater sense of weakness and drained vitality which in turn makes you feel even more helpless. It is similar to the effect after a caffeine high or a sugar rush. It is interesting to observe how attention can be drawn into an area of seeming excitement for a moment. It becomes analogous to scratching the skin when it is dry. You cannot help scratching at the same time that you know you should not be scratching at all. Very subtly, you feel that you have become the victim and you prolong the thought or the distraction, whereas, in reality, you are the one who created it.

Without your conscious knowledge you are very cunning in your own mental mechanisms. You are not victim to the distractions, you create them and follow them through. For example, you may be at a point in life when you are seemingly at ease, and suddenly you find that you are actually bored. People often ask what they can do so that they would need only two hours of sleep a day in order to spend the rest of their time in productive activity. I tell them that this could make them go crazy because they would not know what to do with all of the time that is left over. They would be bored beyond belief. In fact, even now you may not know what to do with yourself and you may be bored and restless, and unable to use what is available to you. Unwittingly, you slowly drift away to fantasies and memories out of boredom.

Viewed in this light, you can see that you are not really distracted by another force. Instead, you create a distraction purposely, though unconsciously, and then you go with it. It is like you are on one railroad track and you intentionally jump to another track. This happens with or without your knowledge and sometimes leaves you wondering where you were before and where you are going now. This is one way in which you try to compensate for something that is not happening right now.

There are still other ways in which you create distractions. Sometimes you have an inability to see certain things. This creates fear, and fear extinguishes your spontaneity. In order to be spontaneous you have to flow naturally and without restriction on your energy. A distraction breaks your supply of energy without your knowledge. You may really want to take off and all systems seem ready. Then suddenly for one reason or another you put on the brakes and tell yourself that something is wrong. For some reason the plane is not flying. You know that the engine is sound and you cannot figure out why it is not taking off. When you look closely at the brakes you applied, you might recognize that there is still a fear of flying within you. The result of this fear is that you applied the brakes. It is in this very same way that distractions occur. Just when you think you truly want to change and move, you find a seed planted in a deep corner, saying "I am not yet ready to mature and blossom. I am not ready to grow." It is important to observe closely what you think the distraction may be saying to you by the form(s) in which it manifests itself. It is similar to dreams or other symbolic interpretations by which you attempt to understand some of your inner mechanisms. In a distraction there are always various symbols showing you ways to return to the correct track. It is through your ability to look at and understand these symbols that you will return to your natural vitality and stability.

The third force is the disturbance that can most deeply alter your life: distortion. Distortions are very, very subtle energies that can come in very friendly ways. They may even come disguised as positive thoughts or affirmations. It is even more important to recognize distortions than it is to recognize attacks and distractions. Distortions are the most subtle forms of energy and can happen in a variety of ways on any occasion. Basically, a distortion is suppressed spontaneity.

When your spontaneity is suppressed, your creativity becomes crippled. The amount of energy that has been held back has to get out in one way or another. Most of the time it goes out in various forms of non-productive thinking which causes disharmony within you. It may manifest in different energies that you see but are unable to accept as reality. One way of looking at distortions is as trapped fear or energy that is blocking the sense of flow or freedom that is always available to us in life.

Distortion is also a force that clouds the clarity of your consciousness. Although it may take on various forms, it comes because of your inability to see or accept things the way they are. The mind creates a triggering, always seeking change. You find that you want to be somebody else, or do something better. Actually, this results in illusory effects, making certain promises within you, saying there is a better land somewhere else or a better thing at some other time. It cripples the forces of energy available to you right now by projecting your own thoughts into a future event or object. Because of the subtle nature of distortions, it is even more important that you be alert and observant. You know that people who have genuinely enjoyed life have really broken the bounds of the known and ventured into the unexplored territory which lies beyond our awareness of the obvious. I call these individuals "warriors."

These people have two major characteristics. One is their childlike ability to see the world and life as it is, and not as it appears according to what we think we know about it. This is the moral of the child's tale, "The Emperor's New Clothes." In this story, when the emperor walks naked through the streets, only a child proclaims him to be without clothes. The rest of the subjects force themselves to believe that the king is royally dressed because they are told that he is wearing his finest new clothes. A child is always naïve, innocent and simplistic. A child always sees the light and not what we see as appearing to be the light. A child sees what is there in actuality and not what he or she is told to see. A child's mind is empty, free of habits, ready to accept, and to be open to all possibilities.

The second characteristic of a warrior is a stability of confidence which he or she maintains within himself or herself. This confidence is not a mental or an emotional energy. This confidence is an expression of the inner strength which allows him or her to speak out, secure in the knowledge he or she has gathered from learning and life experience. The warrior can act only with spontaneity. This type of energy in a person not only flowers internally, but expresses and manifests itself externally as well.

Looking at all three forces -- the attacks, the distractions, and the distortions -- the one thing they share is a resulting sense of unworthiness or a helplessness which creates a barrier to your full enjoyment of life. This immediately triggers a set of thoughts within you which tells you that you cannot attain what you want, or that you cannot be totally happy at any time or that you cannot reach your destination. Most frequently, it hinders the creativity and spontaneity within you and upsets your stability, vitality and clarity. When these vital energies are disturbed you find that the meaning and excitement of life itself becomes distorted. Understanding and becoming aware of the nature of these forces will give you the strength and ability to revitalize and re-establish the energy within you in order to fully appreciate the life within you -- the life with which you can play forever.

"Breaking Reality" and Other Explorations in Consciousness

We are born with the ability for spontaneous combustion
of the fire within that will emit the light of brilliance and
illuminate the world around us in rainbow colors.

"Breaking Reality" and Other Explorations in Consciousness

From Fire To Light

You are naturally beautiful when you are not being interfered with. The beauty of something exists by the nature of non-interference, like a flower in the jungle. There is great beauty that comes along with freedom, or what I call the space that is not polluted by anything. There are no weeds; there is nothing clinging to it. When things are not being pressured by anything else, they exist in the natural state. The reality we normally see is not that of a free space. You feel all things are colliding or are attached or are in confusion, but beyond that is a very open space where things remain in what I call "silence." Silence is not the absence of sound. Silence is truly the space that exists between two points for the mere joy, for the mere wonder, for the mere sweetness of no purposefulness. There is a space that exists that has no specific purpose. If a person is doing this or that for another person, then it is not a very clean space.

We usually see life as collisions of many things, of contrasts. Everything collides; that's a natural part of the motion, anyway. But rather than just a collision of things that we normally see, things also always exist in a space of silence. There are two things happening at the same time. You are fighting with your personal life: your confusion with your loved ones, your job, earning money, and the future. These are all what? Survival issues. Personal space. Personal space is actually what you are always involved with, obsessed with, and completely attached to. You are very, very attached to the personal space, and find it very difficult to break out of it. Because of the nature of the personal space, you do not normally see the space of silence and the space of brilliance that stay around you all the time.

What happens to you when you come and have sessions and play with me is that the personal space gets broken down. Not that you go insane. Usually when you have no personal space, it is almost like not having a reference, it makes you very disoriented; you feel more grounded now. You feel very, very stable, because you are not interacting in a personal space. You are moving into much more -- into a space of silence, into a space of brilliance. What is between two people and what is between you and me is a space of silence and brilliance. It is the way things remain what they are, with no purpose.

A flower did not blossom to make you ignite, or to make you wonder either. A flower is not born for your satisfaction. A rainbow never appears in order to make you feel excited. A rainbow never appears, anyway. You make a rainbow in your perception. In your creation of a rainbow, you put yourself into a state of wonder. Nothing actually comes to life to make you feel good or bad. If that were the case, there would be certain very strict boundaries and a plan, and there would be a beginning and an end. A flower is a flower. A flower does not blossom in order to make you sweet, soft, gentle, or to make you a poet or a botanist. A flower is just a mere flower; a rainbow is just a rainbow. But it is your creation, your perception, your interaction that puts you into a state of sweetness and wonder. And that is actually breaking out of your personal space. Otherwise you do certain things because something will happen as a result. No, you do something only for the pure joy of it. I am not actually with you for you to be awakened or enlightened. Then there would be a motivation and a purpose and a reason in it. Behind everything there is no reason or purpose as such. If you say there is reason and a meaning, it immediately becomes heavy duty. It becomes an obligation. It becomes a goal. This is not for healing your body and mind. Healing is a natural result, however. When you swim, you cannot help getting wet. It is such a joy to be with you, even if you are cranky and whiny. You see, that is outrageous. If somebody can be joyful with you even when you are cranky and whiny, that is great. Otherwise, you are only joyful when somebody is good to you, is giving you something, or is helping you.

The adventure of life begins when you realize you are here for the mere joy of living. Survival has one purpose: the joy of living while you are in it. Not when you are dead; while you are in it. It is not written in the script that you are born to be awakened or enlightened. You are born to die. You change your horoscope before you die. It is not the stars and the planets that control and manipulate you and put you on a course -- the Course in Miracles -- or anything like that. It is really your ability to choose and change that changes the Course in Miracles, so to say, in the planets and the stars. They will be wondering, "What is that woman doing down there?" because of the true nature of your outrageousness that will come out of passion and brilliance. It can also come out of weirdness, rudeness, arrogance, and complete selfishness. But it can happen in a very different way.

For you, being real is being selfish, nothing else. That is why breaking the nature of the selfishness means breaking reality. You think that breaking reality requires Olympic-type achievements. No, it is not Olympic-type achievements that can really break our reality. Breaking reality happens when you can break the selfish nature of the way you see life, the way you possess people. That is what I call the Path of Liberation. The Path of

Liberation consists of breaking out from the non-liberating survival tactics of life. This path is not for everybody. It is only for a few adventurers who see life in its complete brilliant sweetness. The true invitation given by your birth is not to hang on here for the rest of your life, but to see what you can do to break the hanging on. And that is what appreciation means. Appreciation does not just mean being thankful because you feel free; you are rid of the lid. Appreciation is seeing in the deepest gratefulness, without any contrast, what is taking place at every moment. That is the presence of true light. That is fearlessness. Until you can appreciate, there is one thing that can really, really, really touch the pulsation of your heart. It is courage. Courage is the deepest force that you have, the fire, the arousal for life. Until you break into appreciation, your best friend is courage -- the courage to see, the courage to move.

The five qualities of the adventurer are to be alert, ready, willing, open and direct. "Open" and "direct" are appreciations, and "alert", "ready," and "willing" are for survival. They are very great qualities. Not only for the U. S. Marines, but also among the tigers, the elephants, and also for ordinary human beings, they are survival tactics. But if they are spontaneously coming through you, they are not survival tactics. They become sources of deep delight and joy. It is a joy to be alert in life; it is a joy to be ready and willing. It takes only one second for somebody who is not alert to be killed crossing the road. It is a joy and delight to be alert spontaneously like a reflex action. Just crossing the road can be such a delightful experience. Just having a warm bath or shower can be so sweet. You don't have to have outrageous other-side-of-the-world experiences. These little things can be beautiful enough to change your life. But there is something that you always desire to have in one way or another. That is a shock.

The greatest excitement or the greatest, deepest joy comes out of a shock to the system. That is why people take drugs. It is a shock to them. But drugs are not only an artificial shock, they kill the person within. There is nothing in the shock, finally. The true shock is actually losing yourself totally. There is a craving in you to completely lose yourself. You could have lost yourself totally in appreciation, in real reverence, through sex, or in other ways.

The moment you opened your eyes in the morning could have delighted you in such a way; you could have jumped out of bed. My God, you are alive! You did not die last night! That in itself would be such a jolting shock to the system. But it does not feel that way. You take for granted that you will be alive, and you also take for granted that you will have a boring day and will be going to bed at night thinking about tomorrow. This is why all the non-liberations -- catharsis, insight, and the others -- are the opposite of being a shock. They bring you back into a recycling of your own thoughts and feelings.

The true nature of life happens because you have a drive. You want to lose yourself completely. Without losing your sanity or a certain sense of references or the sense of the things you have, you want to lose all the heaviness you have. You never want to have disturbing thoughts. You want to feel free to feel delightful with everybody. No matter how crazy, angry or possessive other people can be, you do not want to be affected by them. You would like to be a hollow bamboo, like a breeze that comes from one end and without any obstructions passes out through the other. You would like to feel like the wind. You would like to feel like a great volcanic fire, at the same time giving warmth. They are real in you. They are not just imagination or fantasies.

They are true human experiences that are built into you in order to explode and evaporate. And that is why you have the ability to even remotely imagine that they are possible. All the things that are possible in the episodes of "Star Trek" and "Star Wars" are little glimpses of truth by the human mind, not the human presence. The human mind can imagine those things.

What you can experience is unbelievable. Science fiction is actually like a child imagining how an adult world could be. You are not a child. Your ability to imagine is very different and also very limited. It is said that we use only one-tenth of our powers, and that is for survival alone. At any time in your life you can be ten times better than this. Half the time you are lazy; half the time you are preoccupied. That is why most things do not happen. Even for a moment if you realize your presence or your capacity to be awakened, it is not ten times greater. It can be fifteen billion times greater than what you are right now. Why fifteen billion times? Because it is nothing personal. That is the space of this, this universe, this cosmos, this energy. This presence of reality is at least fifteen billion years old.

You have at least fifteen billion times the power, because you are actually not part of creation. You are not created as a toy for somebody to see. There is no creator or creation. Do you understand? That is very difficult to get into. You would love to believe you are a creator. You did not create this universe. You would love to believe that, but there is no such thing. The final line is that you are free to go. If you are the creator then you have a responsibility. If you are a creation, then you are a puppet. There is nothing. You are free to go. You are free to move. But you always behave as if you are the creator or the victim. You always behave; you always take a role. Most people like to move around as if they are the creator. You are actually a creator of trouble, not the universe. Somehow or other you do not like the role that you are free to move. Somehow it does not feel to you that you belong in that role. You are free to move like the breeze. The whole beauty about life as play and the light comes into it.

When you have a session, something very interesting happens. Once you are exposed to the Light, it is almost as if you go through the scanning system in the airport. All your psychic powers become null and void. In a sense they are exposed; they do not function anymore. Two students were doing channeling before they met me, and they completely grounded. They spoke in their real voices, not through channels. They became very real. In a sense, what normally happens in a session is that you are reduced to a minimum. You are not expanded to the maximum. You are reduced to a minimum by your exposure to the Light. That is called humbleness. Your ego really shrinks. You know like "Honey I Shrunk the Kids." It is a certain thing that happens to the ego and the mind. When you shrink, you find a very interesting world. It looks so big and exciting now, because you feel very little. But not in a bad way. Exposure to the Light really does not give you any power at all. In fact, it just makes you feel so simple -- but not helpless. Simple in a very, very gentle form, in a very gentle way. When you are reduced to a minimum, you feel much less heavy. Rather than expand, you experience the humbleness out of which comes everything else.

It becomes almost unimportant to do things that you wanted to do before or to prove anything. You have nothing to prove to anybody. It makes you feel a little ridiculous, but in a good way, because it does not leave you with any "show time." Show time disappears. And some people do not like it, so they do not come back. It has nothing to do with any benefits. There are no benefits at all. This is the only place where people pay a hundred dollars and spend two minutes and have no benefits. You must be really crazy. Or else, it may be also very interesting in the way we see value. It is a very different look into life, like an outrageous connection through which you see things. I have various other things that happen, not only the Light. Sometimes people disappear. It is unlike magic.

There is a big difference between magic and mystery, because in magic there are places that you hide and deny. A session with me blows all the places that you have been hiding, so there is no place to hide anymore. You have to make the calls that you have been postponing. So, after the session you will be calling the people that you do not even want to call. In a sense, there is nothing you are trying to hide anymore. Spontaneity, when it happens not by your choice, is very strange. When it comes naturally, it is fine. But when you feel like you are doing something, which seems spontaneous but yet not in a way that is connected, it feels wonderful.

The moment you realize that you are neither the creator nor the creation itself, it immediately releases you from guilt. It cuts the cord of guilt. You feel guilty to have an outrageous life. So you behave, trying to be a good woman. A bad girl is a great example of the adventure of life. When I say "bad girl," there is nothing bad. What I am saying is that outrageousness comes when you feel you are not under obligation to anybody or anything. You do not owe anybody anything at all. And nobody owes you, either. The true nature of life is that the presentation of love is never confined to a source or to a point. We normally think there is a source, and then we become very possessive, demanding and commanding with our lives. It is very outrageous to even imagine the expression of love for life without boundaries -- which is really the true nature of Infinity.

Infinity means there are no boundaries. You are not made out of a unit. You are made out of Infinity. You are actually made out of Infinity, but in order to present yourself in appreciation, you are here as one human being. Just one human being of Infinity. If all of you hold hands and revolve very fast, beyond the speed of light, you will be nothing but Infinity. You will all just dissolve, all your shapes, colors, hair -- all will dissolve. There will be nothing but Infinity. All of you will disappear as colorless, odorless, cool breeze. That is what you are already, but in a different form right now. You are actually playing with the cool breeze, which is yourself. But in order to play with yourself, you have a party here. You have so many human beings. Do you understand?

You are not actually playing with anybody else. You are playing with yourself. You do not normally see it that way. That is why you become jealous, angry and obnoxious. If you really see that you are playing with yourself, it makes you awkward, odd. So you create distinctions in order to accommodate yourselves. Anyway, do not hide. You do not have to think so seriously right now. But that is what magic means. Magic is very simply presented. Magic is just the unbelievable beauty that you are attracted to. You are attracted to colors, shapes, and forms of everything that exists.

Everything that exists puts you into a charged field. Between you and anything that you can see and touch and feel from here is a charged field, like two magnets. Where the two magnets are brought to a certain point a great magnetic current erupts. A charged filed is very simple to understand. A charged field is a space where you cannot sleep, where you are constantly brought back. It is completely alive. But appreciation is not a charged field. The charged field is actually the wonder, the beauty and the sweetness. The beauty about it is that you are attracted to life out of ignorance, out of innocence. That is the way it is. It is not a good or a bad thing. But when you say, "That is the way it is," everything as it is is sweet. Your ignorance is a sweetness. Do you see that? It makes you already humble. It makes you really move toward the Light. The ignorance has a sweetness. Brilliance is not sweet. If you really see, brilliance is tasteless. You may not even want it, because it is tasteless. When I say tasteless, I mean it is a different space. It is not the same taste that you are experiencing right now.

You are attracted only to magic. Everything that is exciting, refreshing, new, is magical stimulation for you. You are attracted to things that surprise you. You are asking every day in life, "Give me another shock; show me another trick; give me another surprise; stimulate me; feed me; touch me in a deeper way that makes me melt by wonder." You are always trying to find them through another human being, through another thing. But although it may be right in front of your eyes, you are always trying to see them in very different ways. Do you see that?

That is the magical attraction. There is always the attraction that naturally takes place. It never dies. But still the very base is ignorance. There is sweetness about not knowing things. Because of the very nature of not knowing things, you are constantly asking for surprises. You are always asking for surprises because there is a base of ignorance that is burning in you, that is yearning -- a deep touch of wonder all the time in your life. One of the deepest joys in life is the moment when you realize the very nature of magic, that it does not leave you anymore to stand and watch. It does not leave you at ease and at peace. Until then, you sit back and enjoy life. Even if there are aliens coming, what you like to do is to have a cigarette and a cup of coffee and to watch them. But if you realize the nature of the way things are happening, your seat in the audience will become so hot you will not be able to sit and watch anymore. You will jump out of it.

The greatest joy of life for the warrior, the adventurer is when he makes the move from the chair to the stage. You are not in the audience, but you are not the actor or the magician anymore. You are only going toward the stage for the pure delight of seeing. You only walk towards the stage then out of appreciation. You sit and watch out of wonder, out of delight. The walk from the chair onto the stage is a walk of brilliance. You are not going to the stage to show off that you are now magic. As you walk to the stage, you feel the presence of the human beings, their innocence, and their delight. You see them very differently. Tears will come out of you with each step you take towards the stage, tears of infinite compassion, tears of infinite brilliance. Even the people who are deeply mean are very innocent babies. If you walk onto the stage, you do not go up and just show magic, you see the audience in complete delight and sweetness. And the greatest magic will be that as you bow, you disappear and find yourself again sitting on the chair where you started. That is the beauty. That is a part of the greatest expression, life. The deepest, deepest joy is a lightness that comes from having no specific requirements of life. There is a very deep presence of lightness that comes. That is very magical.

"Breaking Reality" and Other Explorations in Consciousness

Your mind is the roadway of your consciousness.

Constantly you speed down freeways, cruise winding lanes,

and bump along narrow paths.

Mind Traps are the traffic jams and sudden stops.

"Breaking Reality" and Other Explorations in Consciousness

Mind Traps

The most important thing about life is that you are present, you are here. Otherwise reality or infinity cannot exist; nothing can exist. One of the greatest stories about life is you, that you are here. Your birthday is wonderful because on that day you arrived here. Can you feel it is a wonderful thing that it happened to be you? Forget the Seven Wonders of the World. The wonder is it happened to be you. I mean if you can really feel that, what else are you looking for in life? The fact that it happened to be you is the real appreciation.

Yet one of the most fascinating misinterpretations of life is that you are troubled by your presence here. You feel troubled by your own presence. It doesn't make any sense that you can be troubled by your own being. It doesn't matter how you appear or what you go through, if you are not who you are. You feel the whole trouble is your mind, your body, your looks, or your wealth. You feel you have not enough wealth, not enough good looks, not enough fire and not enough sex. With all of these things, there is a certain sense that you have. The only way you are troubled by your being, directly or indirectly, is you feel trapped. You feel trapped one way or another. Somehow you're trapped not inside the body, but inside this being, inside this life.

What is this "trapped?" For one person it may be ego. The mind says things and has beliefs and conditions. For others of you, it may be a totally different thing. It is personal to each individual. To describe each one of these traps is like trying to describe the same day in different ways. You might describe the day by saying, "Oh, it's a nice day," or "It's a sunny day." You could say, "It's a beautiful, sunny day," or "It's a terrible, sunny day." You might say, "Who cares about sunny, I like the snow!" You describe it in certain ways. It's not that you are wrong. There's nothing wrong about whatever you feel, whether it is a dream or reality. Yet all of these things I am talking about are not the very essence of reality. That's the difference. That is why you feel trapped inside.

Let me illustrate. Say you were born to a very poor family and had hardships, or you were born to a very rich family and had money, and then you blew it. How you see it doesn't matter. Maybe you have physical, emotional or mental limitations. Maybe you have structural dysfunction or other inadequacies. You may have an extremely beautiful face except for your nose. Maybe you lack hair. These are just examples. It doesn't matter. It doesn't matter whatever they are. Also, it doesn't matter about your thoughts or internal dialogues. It doesn't matter about time. They show only one thing. They show what is called the imperfection about life. What you are describing by your not being good enough is imperfection. "Never enough" is just imperfection. What you're trying to describe as a trap is an imperfection of the very essence of life. You are thus blaming or claiming that imperfection is what makes you not such a great person. Do you see this?

However, the imperfection is what challenges you to live life to its fullest at any given moment. Imperfection is the provocation that allows you to say, "Hey, buddy, life is uncertain, so enjoy it." Imperfection is what actually allows you to say, "Hey, I know you are having a great time. You think you are a big shot but, by the way, life is unpredictable." Are you able to see this? Imperfection tells you things in such a way to bring your awareness and alertness to peak times and allow it to remain at a peak moment. That is a most important thing.

What is the difference between a Mafia boss and a sacred man? Both are actually in a state of alertness. The Mafia guy has to be in alertness or he will be shot dead. His life is always hanging around on the edge. A sacred man also is hanging around the edge because he is just seeing what is there. The sacred man is seeing in appreciation and wonder. He is naturally alert. How could he not be alert? This is such a beautiful thing to be at the edge of life always. Back to the Mafia guy. He is at the edge of life because if he is not alert, then his life is threatened. It is two different things. You are actually trying to be both. Do you understand? You are trying to be both like the Mafia boss and the sacred man. You feel like your life is being threatened. You feel you have to be taken care of and careful.

At the same time, you have this sense that there is something else. You have nice, little glimpses about reality. These glimpses add spice into your understanding of things. Somehow or other, you are trying to figure out whether the trap is a dialogue from your mind or gas in your body or your environment. It is actually just the spectrum of imperfection -- the spectrum of unpredictability and uncertainty. This makes life an exciting drama. Then life has a certain edge about it.

For instance, suppose there is an accident. Some cars are traveling along and crash. It's unpredictability. Rather than making it bad, it can be an opening. It can become an opening. It is always how you see it. What I'm trying to say is that you experience a trap by contacts that make you feel, somehow or other, not enough. Somehow you are not enough. You are not experiencing a deep fulfillment. You are not experiencing a complete fulfillment so that you can absorb and just disappear into it. Instead you always feel the trap that is there. The true nature of the trap is not the imperfection. The trap exists because you are not empty. You are heavy inside, and it is because of the heaviness that you experience a trap. You will never feel a trap if you feel light.   If you feel light, you are free. It is pressure you feel.

You experience a trap as a certain sense of pressure. You see, it is pressure that makes you feel you have to break something, have to get out of something, have to come out of your mind or have to come out of limitations.   You feel trapped because of a certain kind of imposed pressure upon your existence -- upon your frame of reference from which you live your life. You experience that pressure because you have anchored yourself with heaviness.   It's like you ate too much. You are bloated now. You are bloated with things that you take or touch and bring into your being by impulses and obsessions.   The consuming feels very pleasurable. But then you feel, "Oh, my God, I'm trapped inside my body and my mind."   Remember, you will never feel a trap if you are porous.   Being "porous" means you feel the lightness. You feel the motion so you do not feel trapped.

This is what happens in the work with me. You experience a certain kind of a take off -- a certain way in which you are carried away without effort. Normally you are making an effort, putting energy into things, expecting something in return.   But, if you can put forth energy and effort expecting nothing in return, then you are truly giving, giving of yourself. This is what I am talking about here.

A trap finally is an illusion. There are no traps that are ever set by anybody unless by yourself. The trap is actually set by you.   It's like somebody took a fishnet, struggled with it, and threw it over himself.   Now he is saying, "Where are the fish? I have to get out of this net first before I can catch the fish."   Do you see this?   It is a trap that is thrown by your inability to appreciate your little imperfections and your little uncertainties.   You are looking for big things and for specific things.   You are looking for big money or for big people.   By "big" I mean a certain way you feel that something can really encompass you, touch you, and take you. This is important to understand because misinterpretation of the trap will cause you to go into emotional cycles -- the emotional cycles of sadness, anger and fear. It is like you are just mad at yourself rather than you love yourself.

At any given point in your life, you have two choices. You can be mad at yourself or you can be in love with yourself. Not just with another man or woman, you have to be truly in love with yourself! When you are in love with yourself, you don't experience a romantic love. You experience the love of compassion for your being and for everything that is there. Whenever you are truly in love with yourself it is not emotional or mental masturbation. It is a freedom of being that actually allows you to feel the bonds that touch everything that exists. This is very important to see how traps come out of the mind, rather than come out of misinterpretations. A true sense about life is that life is like a day-to-day moment. It is not just one moment of glory or grace or anything. A moment of sweetness in your life or in your work can be about meeting a client, a patient, a student or a friend. Part of the uncertainty, especially the imperfection, comes in disguise. Imperfection comes and tells you, "Okay, you have to have this amount. That'll make you fine." You have to remember that your mind is telling you this.

Your mind is telling you, "You have to see this, then you'll know you are fine. You have to get this." Your mind is creating a certain structure. You can't be happy with two hundred thousand dollars you have to have half a million dollars. Then, even half a million is not good enough. That is how people lose in gambling. They win three thousand dollars, but they will not go home. They want to have four thousand. So they try for four thousand, then go down and lose everything. The mind sets you with traps. See that. The mind sets you with traps -- it says you must do this and do that. The traps come as what? They come as goals and projects. Your mind says, "You have to live with this man or woman for three years, then you can talk about what you are going to do." Such goals actually lead into frustration, sadness, anger and fear.

In the beginning you go into a feverish space -- anything that is new, first is very exciting. Whether it is a new job, a new relationship, a new place, it is very refreshing. It is refreshing not only because it is fresh, but even more so because you are moving out of your background. For a moment you don't have a memory and knowledge with this new person, with this new job, or with this new space. It feels to you like you are in a new world. You actually are in a new world because any moment you do not have a memory or a knowledge about yourself, you are in a new world. Any moment that you do have a memory -- data or information-- then you are in a state of heaviness even though you are just remembering flashbacks of the great moments. With all of the flashbacks of the great moments also come little undercurrents. These little undercurrents, which make you emotional and sentimental, have little bubbles of pain and sadness. All of the sweet moments of your life are connected. A word does not exist by itself; it is connected with one in front, one behind. Likewise, you do not have one great moment in life that is not connected with another moment and another. It is a chain reaction. So, although you may remember a moment, it also has two other shadows that are holding it that may not be clearly visible. Always they are there. Nothing exists by itself. Not even a thought, nor even a remembrance, exists by itself. They all come with a big bang, with a family. This is important because in a state of alertness, you can see and enjoy what you are doing right now, and need never ever go back.

"But," you might ask, "don't we need to set goals for work and things like that?" Of course, there are goals. But what I'm saying to you is that you can't be fixated by the goal. You cannot get obsessed by it. You don't play to lose; you play to win.

Although you play to win, the beauty about the thing is that actually you are playing and enjoying the game. I am not referring to play necessarily as a physical game. Everything is play whether you call it office work, law or medicine. All of these are actually connected with ways of bringing about the sweetness. I mean for you to see the structure about this. This is what I am trying to describe to you. The mind sets up something. You are not satisfied. This doesn't mean you have to be satisfied and then lay back and say, "Oh, this is good enough." Or, "Okay, I might just give up." You will never say that. No, you will never give up because of this --- you are greedy, lusty, and craving. It will never be over. But, it is not a bad thing. It is not bad unless you are obsessed or fixated. Nothing is bad! Nothing is bad unless it makes you sick or down. Whether it is smoking, drinking or whatever, if it makes you awake and enlightened, great! But if it actually makes you a fool, if it makes you crazy, sick or tired, then it will be foolish to do it. This is very simple common sense.

In the same way, there are thoughts and feelings that come to you. You see them attacking you. They are just attacks, but also they are traps. There are people who may come into your life. You have to be very alert. New people, new loves, new excitements, new this and that may come. Be alert! Be very alert, especially with new love coming into your life. Don't just go by what it looks like. You have to see what it is doing to you. We draw things into our lives -- new situations, new people, new energies. Life always keeps changing. But then there is a certain way you refuse to enjoy the unpredictability. You refuse to enjoy the impermanence. You refuse to enjoy the uncertainty about life. It is the opposite of what you think makes you feel good. You refuse to see the very nature about what is.

There are only three things that are most pleasurable and very natural about life. Number one is breathing -- just the fact of the breath. Breath itself is opening. With the breath comes the force. Breath is not just breathing in oxygen. Breath comes through the force. It makes you alive. It is sensuousness. Number two is sensuousness.   Everything about life is sensuous. Everything about life is in motion. Number three is realization. Realization is seeing things the way they are. The breathing, the sensuousness and the realization are the three openings of our consciousness, the three openings of infinity.

"Breaking Reality" and Other Explorations in Consciousness

"Breaking Reality" and Other Explorations in Consciousness

When you gamble with your mind,

you lose your body.

Who paid the price?

"Breaking Reality" and Other Explorations in Consciousness

Nature of Reality

There are two things with which you are always in touch. These two things come as light and motion. Motion is actually the sounds, the sounds of motion. I don't mean sound as noises and voices. All of the noises and voices are just dialogues. What is news? News is dialogue. Somebody is telling a story. It doesn't matter if it's fact, fiction or dreams, it's just news. All the stories are there. Melody, however, means tuning into a certain rhythm -- a rhythm that exists in everything. There is a dance in everything; there is a motion in everything. Getting into this rhythm -- this motion -- will create a certain emptiness and silence for a brief moment. Your dialogues change while you are standing and listening to the music. You are touched. There is a certain beauty in this surrender. You give yourself into the sound of music. Or rather, the sound of the music is taking you in. It takes you in. The sound of music is not just the piano, instrument or melody that is there. The sound of music, finally, is your ability to see and feel the wonder that makes you and your life a much more delightful space.

Music has a very interesting way of dismissing boundaries and creating openings. The lightness in the music leads to the realization finally that there are no big deals. But in your mind, there are big deals. There are issues in your mind. There are priorities, contradictions and conflicts. There are all kinds of energies that are moving in the human mind -- in your mind. What is actually moving in your mind is not felt as a point of reference or as mind. As you say everything, you feel it as emotions. You feel it in your heart. You do not actually feel it in your body. These feelings then either provoke your emotions to erupt, disrupt or to open. Like a rainbow, they can evaporate the whole space that is there. In a certain way, you are looking to justify your present arrival here. Your present arrival is not the same thing as your arrival in life. You have arrived at this point in time. It is the declaration of your reality. The interesting thing about this reality is that it is not experienced as a vision, as an interactive intelligence or as a space of recognition, but rather as an emotional space. Every moment of your life is emotional space.

Every moment of your life is like the waves of a great ocean. How the waves look is actually how you feel. What you have are just various forms of tears. When I say tears, I mean that the current of your life is the melting power. It is like the tears are actually going through you. These are not just tears. Do not misunderstand these tears as tears of just sadness. There are tears of sadness. There are tears of joy. There are tears of compassion. There are tears of realization. When I say tears, you are melting, melting into one ocean called your being, which is condensed and put together to create this form -- your form.

Who do you belong to? Who do you love? Any answer that you have is true. Even it you cannot answer or if you say, "I don't know," it is true. The truth of the matter is that, finally, love is not about one person or entity. That is the true nature of the sacred space. A sacred place is not a straight line between two points. It is a circle. You don't live in a straight line between two points. However much you love somebody or however much you may think that you belong, it is not a straight line. It is a circle. That is why in Hindi, they call you rasalila (raz-ah-lee-la). It is like a circle of sweetness, a circle of love. I have a painting in which Krishna is at the center holding a woman. Around him there are seven women dancing. This symbolizes the circle -- a circle of love. The symbolism is not speaking against personal relationships, but rather signifies that anything truly experienced through one person will spread to a circle. It is not a reversible reaction. Love is not just a reversible reaction. It is like music; it spreads like ripples. Love is the ripples if you really have the joy of life. The joy of life comes out of your ability to spread yourself and not hold yourself. This is where the understanding of what is true sacredness comes along.

To give an example, consider when Siddhartha, who became Buddha, left his palace. He could have been a great king, but he left his palace, leaving his beloved wife and baby, the most precious ones to him. He had to be crazy to do that. Why would he actually do that? He did it out of realization, but not only out of realization. There was also an attraction that was brought upon him by a deeper bonding which he felt with the circle rather than with one point, one person. I am not asking you to always feel a great compassion for all beings. You have a list of the people you would rather kill -- not actually kill, but not want in your life.

There is always a certain kind of energy that is there. A good exercise is to draw a circle that represents your universe. Within the circle show yourself at the center and the people in your universe as points, close or far from you. Draw straight lines with arrows to connect you with those in your life. The arrows show the direction of the flow of love and may be one way, both ways or not at all. This circle shows how things exist inside your universe.

Finally, what I am trying to say is that there is nobody you can hold. Also, there is nobody who can hold you. Just remember that. You are free. In all this you are free. Your mind may want to, however, impulsively and obsessively find somebody, seek somebody and hold somebody. Do you understand what I am saying? In human nature you feel good when you lean against someone. When you lean against somebody, it feels pleasurable, very pleasurable. The pain comes with this, though, as a shadow that follows you. There is nothing that you can ever hold, and nobody either. I am not just talking about loved ones. I am talking about anything and everything in life. There is nothing actually you can hold onto. This doesn't mean you just give up, go into the street and become a beggar. Do not misunderstand. The mind will try to sabotage -- will tell you to live, suffer and die. Don't let your mind corrupt you and tell you another story while you are reading this. What I am telling you is actually a supreme teaching about true love. True love is not a personal love. Out of true love is a recognition and a compassion that opens.

Whenever you are having a good time in life, you will be challenged. Either your loved ones will be taken away, creating a space for you to go off-balance emotionally, or new people will be thrown into your existence to say, "Hey, look at this now." You have to see them with alertness, otherwise you are going to pay a price. Because, in any form of excitement, what you can lose is your freedom. If your freedom is lost, nobody can ever give you with any amount of money, sex, or energy, a space filled with innocence and sweetness. Freedom means having a baby-like nature. I am actually a baby. I don't pretend to behave. I don't behave to satisfy other people's judgment. Freedom is a sweetness. Be a baby! Don't try to be an old man or woman. Don't try to be wise and right. There is no wise and right. Be a baby!

Let the baby come out and experience this world out of sweetness. No restrictions. No orders. Then only will you find that your life will become meaningful. You won't have to ask what is the purpose of life because it is meaningful to you. You try to find the purpose and goals of life only when you feel your life is meaningless. When your life is meaningful, you are not after goals, directions or purpose for life. Life is already rich. Your life is meaningful when you have the complete freedom to feel, like the music that comes and touches you. Everything else is voices and noises that tell you, at some point or other, you are here. You are somebody. Behave. The voices tell you this is either good or bad. Throughout your day-to-day lives you are judged in other people's eyes and by other people's feelings. You are somehow or other managing a circus. How can you live that life? Your life does not have to be a circus. You can be like a great skier, just going. In skiing what you experience is, number one, total freedom. But total alertness with the freedom is necessary, otherwise you'll be dead.

I hope you feel what I am saying. I am not trying to educate or inform you. I am just trying to get your little hearts pumping fear, pumping with a certain kind of energy. I want you to come out and see that there is more sweetness. Your hearts are just great, but they are not "brave hearts." There actually is no such thing called brave hearts. There are only brave spirits. If there were a brave heart, it would be one that can transcend a fearful heart. A fearful heart is a heart that is pulsating and making arrangements, making things and making order. This fearful heart can change into a heart of love and sweetness. When your heart is not fearful, it doesn't matter whether you have a surprise visitor in your house or a fish in your tank, they will look the same. I'm not speaking about them literally looking the same. I am saying they will be felt the same way, as sweetness. That is the beauty about it. What I am trying to show you, and have you see, is the background noises that are telling you various things. One way or the other you feel, somehow, you are not good enough. There is a certain version given that you're not good enough and somebody else is a little better than you. Good enough always comes out of contrast. You compare and contrast with or without your knowledge. Always it is there. You can never feel bad without a contrast. You cannot have a shadow without you being there. You can't say, "Hey, whose shadow is that?" It's your shadow. The shadow comes because you look at it. If you don't look at the shadow you won't see a shadow. It is very simple. You will never see a shadow unless you look at it. Without contrast you can never feel bad. What makes you feel bad is a judgment that is thrown into your dialogues that says, "You fail. You are not good enough in many ways."

In any play or any work with me, you are taking off from yourself, from your dialogues. That is why you experience such a freedom and such a delight. Is there a trap here? The trap is that you don't see the trap. When you don't see the trap, you see somebody else outside. Your dialogue says, "Hey, you are making my life miserable," or "You are making my life happy," or "You add something into my life that is great." Nobody adds or subtracts to your life. The trap is made by sounds, made by clouds. Clouds can come and cover the blue sky and say, "You're having a terrible day." No, it's not. Always remember that you are not a big shot. Very simple: You are not a big shot, and if you can realize that, most of the time your life will be fine.

What you are doing with me is, in fact, removing the fat of your consciousness. The fat actually feels good when it is there, but eventually it kills you. The sessions, practices and journeys that you do, are melting layers away letting you becoming lighter. Of course, you are fighting with it at the same time, but that's a part of the whole nature. It is like you are unlearning everything. You are unlearning all of the beliefs and conditions, all of those things, that made you feel like somebody. When you unlearn, the ego goes into panic. The ego says, "Hey, what are you doing? You are killing me." You are telling yourself you are nobody. You are realizing you are nobody. That is very stimulating and very frightening at the same time. There is a certain sense -- an energy -- that is lifting in you which is the most sweet energy, or it can be a frightening energy. Becoming open means you are becoming vulnerable. Becoming open is like a Mafia boss who suddenly decides to go walking on the street by himself. He's vulnerable and not at ease. Then there is the man who is at ease walking on the street. He doesn't give a damn about anybody. He doesn't give a damn about whether others notice him or not. He doesn't care. This is not out of rudeness, but out of sweetness, that he doesn't care.

When you are vulnerable and not nervous, you feel absolutely great! Be vulnerable! Vulnerable means being on the edge. Be on the edge of your consciousness. I am not saying to put yourself into some kind of danger by running across the road. No, not at all. I mean for you to stay humble and for you to stay with what you have right now. Humbleness means that you stay and acknowledge what you have, not what you don't have. You see the little bit left in a glass, not the whole empty glass. You see differently. You have something right now. Do you know what you have? You have a damn good life. What you have right now is actually a damn good life. Don't blow it. You may have a list of the things that you don't have, but that's not what life is. Right now, still you have a damn good life. You are living damn good. You can actually stretch that and become a very beautiful luminous light. It is out of this imperfection -- it is out of this uncertainty   that you will rise.

Life is an ocean of love with never-ending waves of light

that illuminate the wonder and the sweetness of life.

"Breaking Reality" and Other Explorations in Consciousness

The Motion of Love

What is the deepest joy of life? Consider this: Your bladder is full; you have to go to the bathroom. Somehow you wake up aware you have a full bladder. But when you go to the bathroom, you have very little pee. You felt, however, you had a very big one. Do you hear what I'm trying to say? There is always in human nature something we feel we have to release. What do we release? What do we think we have to release?

I'm trying to come to what is called surrender in a different way. All the work we are doing right now is about surrender. Life is actually nothing but surrender. You are out of touch with life, which is why you are having trouble with it. You are not in the track with life. You feel you are, but you are not. It doesn't matter that you are having a good life, that your life is not falling apart, so to speak. So you feel good about things, but is life really good?

What is surrender? What is really totally giving? Can you outrageously make a step and give what is precious to you to touch someone who is very dear to you, not just for you and not just for your life? Will you do that? You have to see that, because within ourselves we have various things we want to release. Whether you actually release or not doesn't matter. It is not like you have to release so you will be empty. That is an illusion. Releasing never makes you empty. Rather, it gives you the capacity to absorb more and fill up. It only gives you the capacity to collect more.

Releasing does not mean something becomes empty. Emptiness comes when you cut the source. When you cut the base -- the source -- only then can you become empty. You can't empty anything by giving out what you have. Cut the base if you want to be empty. Then there is nothing to hold on to. Cut the base.

What is the base? First we need to get in touch with what the realization is here. The realization is that we feel like we have to release something. It comes out as dialogues; it comes out as sadness; it comes out as tears; it comes in temper tantrums; it comes in panic attacks. You can name it in so many ways, ways how you feel you have to release. But do you feel empty when you release in these ways? No. You get exhausted when you release. The moment of exhaustion feels like, "Oh, yeah, I feel better." That is a certain kind of release -- it is an urgency that we feel. We feel that we just want to release something that is troubling us.

Remember, first of all, you feel you have to release something because something is troubling you. If something is not troubling you, you want to hold on to it. You like to keep it. Somewhere always we feel there is a need to release emotions, words, or energy. People do all kinds of things to try to release-- they sweat in the body; they sweat in tears; they sweat in emotions and dialogues. They have a restlessness.

There is another sense that we experience with release. It is a sense of loss. With release, we also experience a sense of loss. We lost someone. We lost something, something very precious. Or if we have not lost, then we have a sense we might lose something. We may lose something or someone. You have an emotional energy like a click of the clock -- click, click, click. You have a sense either that you have lost somebody or something that is very precious. What do you feel then? Restlessness?

Sadness? Anxiety? You feel a sense of emptiness, but that is not emptiness as a silence or a space. You feel empty like, "Blah!" You feel empty like, "Who cares? I don't care whether I live or die now." Then your mind will say, "Psh! It's true. Here is a real list of things I lost. It is true." Then a list comes, like a flagship, a list of things you have lost. "Poor me, poor suffering me!," says your mind.

Another sense is the fear that you are going to lose somebody or something. You have to see this very clearly. You have this sense of loss, and it doesn't matter whether or not it is something or somebody very precious, and if it has happened or just might happen.

That is where you are. You are not standing for no reason; you're not standing because life is unbelievable; you are not standing out of appreciation or out of wonder, or to see the humble nature of existence. If it were so, you would not be experiencing the other undercurrents of emotional energies. These are undercurrents; they are not actually conscious. They come and just touch you. What you feel is not in your mind but in your body. You don't feel sadness just in your mind. There is no such thing called sadness and fear experienced by your mind. Fear and sadness are experienced in your body. Likewise, when you feel very happy and alive, it is your body that feels it. There is a certain rush that goes through you. Without your body you don't feel anything. Without your body, you actually have no way to view life. You are just a ghost then. This is not about ghostbusters. This is about real life and about realizing the meaning of surrender.

That is where the whole beauty comes about life, because our life is constantly challenged. Our life is constantly challenged by surprises and by changing detours that allow us to change the very nature of our planning and scheming. You are actually miserable because your life is not happening as you want. It is very simple. You are not miserable because life is so bad. It's not that bad. You have basic goodness; you have food on the table; you have work; you have friends. But you don't experience them to the fullest. You are not in touch with the deepest intimacy because the undercurrents come and disturb you. They actually don't let you experience the nature of silence, the nature of sweetness, which is in your heart. The undercurrents come in little ways. Your mind is drifting here and there.

Do you follow what I'm saying right now, because it is important to understand this before we can think about the question, "What is surrender?" or "What is giving in?" or "What is love?" or "What is connection?" Finally, there is no such word as "connection" or "surrender." You can call it "oneness," the oneness with everything, which is the beauty about life. So the base line, the thing to first see, is that we have always a certain energy that we feel we need to release. It is almost like a reflex action within you, like you're always trying to vomit. You're trying to throw up something. It is like you have swallowed something unnecessarily, or swallowed something that is a foreign thing to you. So you just want to get it out of your system. What is this thing you want to get out of your system? What is this truly about? What are you telling yourself? It is this: if you can change something, if you can do something different, then you will be okay.

We always believe there are alternatives to our life. We feel there are certain things that can be added or subtracted. But, all these things that are added or subtracted, will they give you more pleasure?

The emptiness is not actually emptiness coming out of any sort of release, even if you are screaming or crying. Mostly, screaming and crying are not just about the losses. Behind the losses is a certain sadness, and behind the sadness is anger and fear of the very nature of your being. There is a certain way in which you are angry at your very own nature and essence. Along with a list of the things that are very real to you that you lost, is a list of the mistakes you made. There are a bunch of mistakes you made, not a tremendous many, but still it is quite a list.

Even so, you have a confirmation somehow that your life will be okay. It won't be an absolutely wonderful, great life, but you have an assurance or an agreement within yourself that your life will be okay. You're not going to suffer too much. It doesn't say in your script that you are going to have an absolutely wonderful, outrageously great awakening or a great life. It tells you your life is to be a limited one, and that is what your sadness is about. There is a certain voice that is telling you about the limitations of your expansion. There is a certain way your dialogue, your voice, is telling you that this is the way things are with you, with your dear ones, and with everything.

One of the greatest joys about life is breaking the cause and effect. Breaking what looks real. Breaking actually what appears as reality. Breaking this script, this voice, this inner dialogue.

Reality says, we are born, we die. No. You can change everything. In appreciation and respect only, you can change. Out of love only, you can change something. The whole idea about surrender is that, truly speaking, you will find release. But, surrender is the most impossible thing in life. For example, you believe you are totally in love: "Oh, I love somebody. I have given myself. I'm with him, and this is great." But, sorry, being in love doesn't mean you are there. You are there, but you are not one hundred percent there. You can't be. You can never be there exactly one hundred percent. If you truly give one hundred percent, then there is always an overflow.

That's actually what true awakening is -- it is the overflow. It is life overflowing. In human life, what we experience with another human being is the personal level. But, if it goes beyond the personal level then there is an opening, an awakening, and that is what I would like to see. That is what I am trying to achieve with people who are very dear to me and who are working with me. I am trying to break the appearance of reality -- the personal space -- to create a space of overflow.

Right now, you are not actually ready to have a realization of this. But the understanding is giving you direction. It is giving you a provocation. Many times you have thought you understood some person. Then you realized you didn't really know them. They were different than what you thought. It is the same with you. Saying it in a different way, what I am trying to do is to give certain poisons to your mind. But this poison is not going to kill your mind. Rather, this is like homeopathy -- a little dose that will activate you in a certain way. My talks are like homeopathic doses to your consciousness. They are little doses of poison that will cut what is necessary to be cut and leave the rest of the space for brilliance and creativity to happen. It will destroy the darkness and the sadness within your life. However happy you seem, you are sad and upset. But the sadness or upset feeling is in disguise. I don't mean that you are sad or upset with me or with family. Here, you are fine. But when you go to the outside world, when you go on the street, you are a different being. You are totally different; you are street smart. You are trying to prove something, trying to show someone, or trying to be somebody. You behave! Here you don't behave. When you don't behave, that's good. It is the only space where you can really experience something very real. That is what we are doing.

All the teachings are like poison to the mind. You love what I say, but you don't like it inside. You love it and you don't like it. You can love somebody but not like them. This is in that same category. Let's come back into the truth of what is. There is the sense of a need to release. You want to talk with yourself about yourself, about how great your life is. How you feel trapped one way or another. How you wish things would be different. There are so many ways in which you can feel it. But every time you feel this, it is a call in your life for you to break the resistance and to give in. It is not just a call, it is a force, a force of attraction. If you can feel this force of attraction, then you are on the right track. Usually, however, you don't feel it. Usually you only feel a force of attraction when you fall in love, or have a sensuous, emotional or physical attraction. You can feel that also with nature. You can be taken by the awesome beauty of the mountains around Las Vegas, or the vibrancy of a sunrise or sunset, or the sweet song of birds, or the majesty of a tree. There is a certain way we feel. Suddenly, we are being taken out of ourselves.

We don't think that way. When your thinking disappears, you recognize something. When you recognize something you feel, in a certain way, attracted by a force. But these attractions have a certain object, whether living or not. There is a certain point of reference you are attracted to.

So there is always a gap between you and another person or you and the mountain. You feel beautiful love; you feel a song; you close your eyes and you feel wonder. There is a certain force you experience, but there is also always a reference point. This feeling is in reference to something.

True surrender is not about another human being. It is not about the mountains. It is not about the trees. It is not about anything. If you can feel a force of attraction, without any reason, without anybody, without a reference point, then you are actually with the force. You are with a force that is lighter than anything that is. Right now your attraction puts your body into body heat. It ignites you. It actually allows you to illuminate that which is around you with a glow you enjoy.

This is actually leading into appreciation and humbleness. When you are attracted and there is nobody there and there is nothing there, that is surrendering. That is, actually, true love.

In true love, the force is so intense that it dissolves the person and the object. Right now you actually do not dissolve. When you love somebody, you hit something and something comes back to you. You enjoy what is coming back. When you love somebody, whether it is a human being or a mountain, a sunrise, a butterfly or a song, something comes out of you. It is a ray of light, a ray of heat. It comes and hits the person. But what makes you feel good is not the hit. What makes you feel good is what comes back to you and hits you back. It is like a swing, like swinging. In true surrender, nothing comes back to you. Right now, you enjoy everything that is coming towards you. Everything!

When you love somebody you feel good because you don't just love, the love comes back. But the interesting thing is that when it hits the person, it comes back as a counterclockwise force. That's why you don't feel time. When you are in love, you are in a counterclockwise force. That's why you don't feel tired. That's why you don't feel irritated. It leads you into a space of greatness. But in true love, there is nothing coming back counterclockwise. There's nothing coming clockwise either. The force will dissolve the object of recognition. Right now you don't want to let the object of recognition disappear! You want to hold it. You are frightened that if the object is not there, there will be no love. If she is not there, then there will be no love. If he is not there, there will be no love. If there are no mountains, if the land is bare, if there is no sunrise, if there is no moon, if there are no stars, what will you see? You are frightened to let it go away. In fear we hold everything. In fear we hold on to this reality. That is actually how we hold, how we create, this reality. We hold it out of fear.

See if you can understand what I am saying. When you love somebody, when you love anything, your thoughts disappear. You see things without a barrier, you see things without restriction, effortlessly, and without friction. It is almost like having no contact. That is why you feel closer. Whenever you love anything, it feels very close to you. When you love someone, they feel very close to you. When you sing a song, whether it is from forty years back or right now, you feel very close to whatever it is. But when you surrender, there is no distance or time at all. There is total disappearance. That is actually the true music of life. We can really hear it, but not through our ears, and not even through our being. The sound is not coming from anywhere. It is just there and you are there. This sound is not coming from a speaker; it is not coming out of an instrument; it is not coming out of anything. It is not even coming out at all! It is just there, an exposure. You are totally exposed. That is the invitation here: the invitation for you to come out.

When I talk to you I am just showing you something. These are not talks to educate you. This is poison, but it is good poison because it is going to show you something. You are going to have a response -- not a reaction -- to what you see! You react to everything. You react to everything in life. I want you to respond. Response is natural like a reflex action. You don't think, it just happens. You can't think and realize. An accident will break through you. Either you will go insane totally, or you will feel very free. Both are the same, except for one thing. With insanity, you will be out of reality. With the other, you will be with reality. You will bypass the thin line of insanity (there is a part of you that is almost crazy) and then it will open a passage for you.

True love comes not with the person and not with any-thing. But do not think that you can actually just feel it without a person right now. A person appears so that you do not sabotage and go crazy. The person is just a gateway, a little gateway, a lit-tle circular gateway. If you come and stand in front of me, in the right moment, automatic doors will open and you can go in to the other side. I say, "automatic doors" because you cannot see the other side. It is like looking in a one-way mirror. Right now, what you see is a reflection coming out of your background. Everything you see in life is just your background. Everything that is happening, like in a one-way mirror, is just the way you see. It is about you. Everything! In this mirror, your eyes have to meet your own eyes. Why do you think I ask people to sit in front of a mirror and look into their own eyes? It is so that one day, when you see yourself, when you see your own eyes, they will pull you out of yourself into the other side. You will take yourself to the other side, which is actually the breaking point.

I want to say your bladder will never be empty. The pleasure is not a release of pressure. Pleasures don't come by releasing pressure. Pleasure never comes by releasing pressure. The pleasure comes by falling. If you can fall and never fear that you will hit, you will fall effortlessly. Falling is a way of surrender. You're not falling now. You are holding on, in other words. You are holding. Your life is in a holding pattern. Holding! But I just gave you the way the picture really works. I let you see it. I saw in your hearts and in your eyes that you were getting a glimpse of what it really is. What it is to truly love, and how it moves.

This talk was about the motion of love. The motion of love is our first introduction into the sacred life. I would like you to take a moment of your time to sit in front of a mirror and just have a little dialogue with the person in the mirror. Have a little dialogue with the person in the mirror about your wanting to release. Just talk to the person in the mirror, as though the person in the mirror is your best friend. Just talk.

One of the greatest joys in life is a moment of appreciation. But it becomes joyful only if you can really truly feel it is there. One of the greatest pleasures is a sacred realization of the very humble existence of life itself. The realization is not about losses and gains. There is a presence you feel that is a very sweet joy. You are living in a living consciousness, in a living space, in a living existence. You are present. Life itself is radiant and joyful, and there is nothing else.

Sadhu.

"Breaking Reality" and Other Explorations in Consciousness

Liberation comes not from releasing stress,

nor from moving out of darkness into light,

but rather from opening your being

into a space of freshness and brilliance.

Nine Wheels of Liberation

The best discourses, whether it is by Christ or a Buddha or any awakened one, were never given to a group of people who were serious. The best talks by Jesus or Buddha were after-dinner talks. After dinner is the best time.

Great religions, great awakenings, or the search for survival, or the search for beyond survival, came as a result of three fundamental provocations. They came as a result of fear, ignorance, and desperation in the human nature. There have been many times on the planet Earth that great awakened ones, or great enlightened ones, have come and delivered messages or shown certain pathways to enable human beings to attain peace, joy, and supreme harmony. But also, they kept a little secret path that was not just about peace, harmony, or serenity. It was about breaking even the peace and the harmony and the serenity into final liberation and realization. It happened throughout the history of mankind.

The enlightened ones gave a clue or a direction for people to see that would bring about a deep joy to the multitude of human beings who were suffering out of fear, ignorance, and desperation. Such were the great Buddha's Eightfold Noble Path and the Ten Commandments. In many ways they helped people to live without destroying themselves. Before you are awakened, you may sabotage so heavily that any chances of awakening or realization may not even touch you, because you would be destroyed by yourself in many ways.

Tonight I share with you, a little gathering of sweet, innocent people-brilliant and not so brilliant -- who this Tilak is and what he has brought onto the earth, which may be known as the Path of Liberation. When I say "not so brilliant," it is not that you are stupid. "Not so brilliant" is actually what is waiting to come out as brilliance. If you were already brilliant, I would not be able to talk to you. Then we would communicate in silence completely. Thank you for letting me have the pleasure of verbalizing the pictures in a way that perhaps you may be able to relate to one day.

Tonight I will introduce to this sweet, innocent gathering the first seven steps of the Path of Liberation. Two shall remain unknown to you until the time when the first seven are digested in you and you may be ready to hear more.

What did the Ten Commandments and the Eightfold Noble Path do for the human being? They gave a set of guidelines and rules. The Buddha spoke about what is called the Middle Path. He spoke about right understanding. "Right understanding;" just see the words. They are a provocation indicating that most of the time you may misunderstand what you see. For what reason? Because you take everything for granted. Most of the time you misunderstand what life is. Then, there is "right speech." You cannot just speak. You cannot just use words. There is something called "right speech." "Right action." There is a right action; and the right livelihood, the job that you do. "Right effort." You may be using the wrong muscle to open your eye. You may be in such hypnosis that you are using all the wrong motions except for the one right effort that may open your eyes. "Right effort." And "right mindfulness" and "right concentration." They were great. The Eightfold Noble Path. The Ten Commandments.

The whole idea is that they gave guidelines, but also that they were introduced while the Buddha was living, while Moses was living. When the Buddha was living, it was not actually necessary for people to go through them. It is when the Buddha will die that the paths will prepare the other human beings and will ready them for the arrival of the next Buddha. Any path is a preparation so that the chosen few, so to speak, will be there one day when the sunrise really comes about.

But the fascinating thing is that the Eightfold Noble Path or the Ten Commandments is never truly understood, is never truly practiced by anyone. They cannot be practiced without the true transmission of the Light that would come from a Living Light itself. When the Light is not real, anything else that is practiced is not a definite transmission. It is called mitya samadhi. It is an artificial, hypnotic transmission. A transmission can take place only through something that is living and not through a conceptual understanding of any kind.

The pathways of the past were great, but they are outdated. They are like a ticket for a great cinema. You have the ticket, but it is out of date. This is a different time. Human beings have become the sharpest, shrewdest, most skillful, brilliant living force in the whole universe. The brilliance is manifested as away of coping with and mastering death and destroying understanding about death. The only way the brilliance is tested by the agents that are invisible to you is by how you deal with death. Human beings have, through the advancement of technology, science, and medicine found various ways to fool death and prolong life. It is only at a time when the human being has the potential -- whether you call it social, spiritual, or psychological -- a certain energy coming from his or her creativity and intelligence allowing one to see what life is and what death is, that it is possible to have a chance of breaking those realities. This is such a time. I have been with you for a couple of years, and some of you have been with me very recently. It was interesting for me to see what was taking place for you. Especially in the last few weeks, I saw the true nature of your restlessness, the true nature of your vulnerability, and the true nature of your violent anger, which perhaps now is so matured that it can come out of you as wisdom rather than as violence. I saw many little games being played among you. Whenever those games are being played, I usually just look around and see the other side. But also, I see your abilities, your true innocence behind it, trying to participate in total merging.

All the fights are about what? Finally, merging together. Your inability to merge as one leads to conflict. You are restricted in many ways. You have had sessions, you have listened to me, you have made many life changes, but yet you will be challenged to see your true, total relationship with me. There are many ways in which you have been suppressed, many fears you have, many ways in which you are restless. When you talk with each other, what do you really talk about? Very simply, you talk about nonsense. What is nonsense? Nonsense is all the things that happen in your life.

Why do you want to talk about your life? Because you have a desire to vomit. Why do you have a desire to vomit? Because you have an inner restlessness. If you are really happy with a person, you have nothing much to say. You are in a state of stillness. There is a way in which you engage yourself without your knowledge and with your knowledge. In order to engage, you bring nonsense into the picture. I will not ask you to have right understanding and right speech, which are beautiful and which can be helpful for your survival. But I am going to speak now about five great forms of liberation and four infinite contacts that make up the Ninefold Path of Liberation.

The first form of liberation will be liberation from catharsis.

The second form of liberation will be liberation from insight.

The third form of liberation will be liberation from order.

The fourth form of liberation will be liberation from technique.

The fifth form of liberation will be liberation from discipline.

Those five liberations will take you out of your body and your mind and bring you into the presence of Infinite Light. First I will talk about the five liberations, and then I will go into the four contacts of Infinity.

The first liberation is liberation from catharsis. All your life you cry and laugh and rest, and cry and cry again and rest. Catharsis is like a flushing system. There have been times I have asked students not to cry even if they wanted to. As a result, a change occurred in their bodies. This is not to say you may not feel sad at times. But liberation from catharsis can happen only when you no longer relate to your past. Liberation from catharsis is a realization that nothing significant ever happened in your life. Your mind will make up many stories; your mind will create many things. Liberation from catharsis means not going back anymore to find out what happened, no more speaking about "this happened to me," no more trying to clear yourself.

As I speak, human beings are getting ready for this. I recently saw an article about a fascinating new form of psychotherapy that is being practiced now by about five hundred therapists. It is called "psychology of the mind." When patients come to these therapists, they do not probe into their problems. In the first session the patient talks and expects the therapist to ask questions. But instead, the therapist tells the patient storie-- stories about the human mind that give the patient a glimpse of realization and bring him into a deep space of wonder. The article described a couple who wanted a divorce. The therapist just talked about how the mind is like a car and the direction it is going in. The wife suddenly got a glimpse of what he was saying and completely broke out.

Catharsis is one way you confirm to yourself that you exist. Catharsis is one way you reconfirm your guilt and pain. Provoking and bringing your pain to the surface will never make it go away. It is an illusion to think that it will. Catharsis is a way the mind always flashes back and claims the importance of events and issues. It creates the ego and brings it to the battleground.

Liberation from insight, on the other hand, is another way in which you restrict yourself by trying to understand what has happened to you. As if understanding could lead you into a different freshness. Understanding not only does not lead to a different freshness, it brings you into a deeper depression -- to the point where your unworthiness comes into greater play and hooks you into another boundary. The insights create boundaries. All the insights reflect back and give you feed-back. Insight brings you to a point where you can promise yourself that you will never, ever do something, only to repeat your mistakes and feel more regretful, more repentant, and more deeply anguished about your life. Liberation from insight refers not only to the personal insight that you carry as a weight, but liberation from knowledge of any kind that you carry.

All the knowledge that you have is dead knowledge. It does not have potency; it is just data that you carry one way or the other. The true nature of insight is that there is nothing to understand about yourself.

Liberation from order is your attempt to put yourself in harmony. You are always trying to bring about a point of equilibrium, a point of harmony, in the illusion that there is a resolution that can take place. Liberation from order brings you into the realization of your life as Light without a solid boundary of any kind. Because of your inability to understand the nature of Infinity, words such as order, balance, harmony and equilibrium exist. They are only mental concepts. It really brings you into a much greater sense of freshness and freedom to know that you do not have to keep an order with yourself. It is not actually disorder, but a deep realization of respect that brings you into knowing that no energy or effort has to be made all the time to maintain a certain kind of sanity, image or role.

Actually, the first three liberations are interconnected. Most of the time you are wasting your life by traveling back and forth between the past and the present. However you may refer to it, it is just the emotional and mental resonance of going back and forth. It is very, very tiring. Your energy is wasted and you feel exhausted, because the life force is actually in motion. It is in one direction. You are interfering by thinking about the past. The moment you think about your life in the past, you have interfered with the spontaneity of the expression of life. The moment you think, you adopt your life in the past, you have interfered with the natural process of the openness of life. The moment you choose to argue, to justify by saying "this happened to me" or "you are to be blamed," you are wasting your life.

Whatever reasons you give, whatever the catharsis you are trying to produce, it is not going anywhere. So much energy and effort have been spent. Any moment you are thinking about your life -- what has happened -- you have a great presence of seeing things without bringing and provoking other memories. To see that is very important. Also, the basic restlessness and nervousness in a person actually brings about the pain and is sadomasochistic. All the forms of catharsis are not only painful, they are sadomasochistic pleasures. They are the ways in which the ego gets pleasure by seeing your defeat. You are the one who is actually doing it; there is a part of you that is enjoying the death that is taking place in you. There is a part of you that is so angry with yourself that it is killing you all the time and enjoying it, too.

Any time you go back into the past, you have interferred with the spontaneous presence of Light that is unfolding, breaking time in your body. Your body is actually the only entrance to an invisible form that you have, that you never knew before, that you had a sense is there somewhere. There is a beauty about this presence of the human body that you have, because the true form of who you are and what you really contain is invisible. Catharsis will never allow you to identify and see the invisible form that is you. Because this physical form itself will get so beaten up and exhausted, it will never become a door. It will become a garage of some kind.

Liberation from catharsis and liberation from insight will already free you, if you understand those two things. And liberation from order. Liberation from order is your attempt to maintain in every way. In order to maintain, you do various things out of skillfulness, out of human manipulation. That is why the fourth liberation is liberation from techniques. You drop all the techniques that you have when you know there is no order. If you have the realization of no order, it is a deep delight to the system. "Oh, now I can rest in peace." When you really understand there is no order, you can rest in peace. Sweet peace.

Techniques are skillfulness used not as skillfulness but as total manipulation geared to bring the rest of the world to your fingertips. All the skills you have used from your knowledge, from your charisma, from yourself, allow you to live like a person in a circus. You are like a clown who has learned a certain trick of the trade and displays it to get all the attention. But behind this clown or circus man is a very sad person. Clowns may make the whole world laugh but cry all alone in the bathroom, and the bedroom, too. The techniques that have been used are the ones that finally kill your complete spontaneity, because all the techniques you are doing are artificial and mechanical. The true essence of the expression of life, all the skills, all the energies that you are expressing, will change into a different form. We will go into detail about that later.

The final liberation is liberation from discipline of every kind. When everything else fails, you impose discipline. There is no discipline. Discipline is a master manipulation to get something that you do not have the guts to get in complete openness and clarity. Discipline is one way in which you cheat yourself, because you do not have the true courage and the sweetness and openness to do it face to face, heart to heart. To liberate yourself from discipline means to liberate yourself from law and order. Discipline actually means law and order enforced for your safety, enforced to keep you going, without which you may destroy yourself. But, truly, it has saved you in a very artificial, superficial way. These five forms of liberation are not for your survival. Those who want to survive, please do not practice this. This is to liberate yourself from survival. This will break your survival. You will break your catharsis; you will break your insight; and there will be no order and no techniques and no discipline.

You only have to know these words today. You do not have to try to understand or get them into your body yet. It will be difficult right now. Just remember it. The first five unfoldings are the ones that finally will break the boundary. That is why I call it the "Fifth Force." The Fifth Force is the liberation of catharsis, liberation of insight, liberation of order, liberation of techniques, liberation of discipline. And there are no walls. There are no walls because, finally, nothing actually happens in your mind. Nothing happens in your body. You will never realize anything at all through your body or mind. Your body and mind were just entrances for you to contact what is life, just as you had the idea about God in order to communicate with the unknown and the Invisible. You use the body in order to relate in many ways. If you want to truly liberate, the lids must be taken off those five forms.

The contact of silence, the first of the four infinite contacts, is not a suppression of sound. It is the zone of total oneness where there is no contact through any time or friction. All the things that I am saying are about breaking from time, are truly speaking the infinite stillness. It is not that you will not be moving, or that you will be glued in place, or that you will not be talking. In the stillness is the spontaneous overflow of gratitude. You can only be still by a force of gratitude. You can only be still with the force of innocence. You can only be still with the deepest humbleness. There is no love as such that exists. All love is just self-love. All your love is conditional and nothing else. But the beauty about human nature is that when you marry or when you love, you will love beyond yourself. And that is the true nature of the appreciation that will come. Until then, in the name of love, in the name of marriage, in the name of families, you are using and adapting people for various neurotic needs that you have to fulfill. You are born with a bottomless pit called craving, which will never, ever be satisfied. No passion will ever be satisfied, because there is a fever behind all the passions that exist. When you liberate from catharsis and insight and order, it is not that you are becoming a saint, but you are actually experiencing life in a very different presence, without sabotage. The way you sabotage is by catharsis and insight. You like to think that catharsis and insight are useful to you, that they help you. But they have destroyed you, stabbed you, and brought you to the point of no mercy as declared by your mind.

The space beyond catharsis, beyond insight, beyond order, beyond techniques and discipline is a space of liquid light -- liquid in the sense that you are melting. There is nothing to hold it or to carry it out. Liquid means your ability to really flow. Liquid means a form of transmission that can take place from one body into another, the contact of silence, or stillness, is the sixth form of liberation. But rather than it being a liberation from something, it becomes a contact. It becomes a contact now, because it is not a liberation into something else. It is a liberation into a contact of humbleness, the stillness.

The seventh is the contact of brilliance. The whole context of the Eightfold Noble Path is a release of -- in one word -- brilliance. Right speech, right attitude, right effort, right mindfulness, right concentration, all chopped and blended together, will come out in one color as infinite wisdom. Brilliance is pure seeing, infinite wisdom.

There are two more contacts that I shall share with you at the right time, right place, in a different space. There are nine points in this Path of Liberation. It is lighter and much more intense than you realize right now. It is not that you do not have the ability to understand what I am saying. You are able to hear what I say, but are not able to completely process it. And it is not necessary right now. This is only the menu; you have not yet eaten the food. I will prepare it and give it to you slowly in a way that will be edible and very tasty. But this is just the menu containing these seven items tonight. I am trying to describe to you what the path of freedom is. It is very difficult to describe. I have had to create a certain way for you to relate to it.

This is the path of freedom containing the five forces: catharsis, insight, order, techniques, and discipline. You destroy them and you shall not survive. Jay Moreno wrote the book about psychodrama called *Who Shall Survive*. It is beautiful -- all about catharsis and therapy. I should say, who shall not survive will be you. If it is about survival, please indulge yourself in insight and in catharsis and maintain your life somehow or other. For the rest of your life it will be a fascinating survival. The only other choice you have is to really know that by nature, you were born rebellious. The only thing that you are not expressing are those rebellious qualities and the force of life you have. Your weaknesses are not truly weaknesses. Your tiredness is not because you have done so much in life. Your weariness is an expression of your desperate attempts to be outrageous and your inability to do so. And the beauty about life is to really see that it is worth giving.

When I say that catharsis and insight are non-personal and are illusions, it is important to realize that life does not include your personal past. It will be difficult for you to get it at once. You are here to see, to understand life. But you are touching yourself; you are totally in love with yourself. You are not in love with life; you are in love with yourself. That is why the five liberations will help you to break self-love. You are obsessed with yourself and that is why you hate yourself.

You hate yourself because secretly, obsessively, you are in love not with anybody else, but with yourself. And you are so frightened that it will go away, that somebody will take it. That is the presence of the ego.

Your body never related to any path, like the Eightfold Noble Path or the Ten Commandments, as a reality. But you do understand about catharsis and insight and order. You know exactly what I am talking about. You cannot say that you love your neighbor as yourself. You hate your neighbor. Even if you think you can love, it becomes artificial and superficial. Even if you have the right understanding or the right effort, your mind will argue, "Right understanding; there must be wrong understanding. Right effort; there must be... You can always argue, rationalize, justify and destroy the paths. The Ten Commandments and the Eightfold Noble Path have always been destroyed by human arrogance and ignorance. But what I am telling you cannot be destroyed, because it is the way you appear when you see yourself in the mirror. Tonight I have shown you just the menu. Next time I will bring the prices and samples for you to taste, and then you will see.

The Path of Liberation is to liberate yourself from two things: your mind and your body. You do many things to your mind and body. If becoming very, very healthy would wake you up, you would already have found a way. Some yogis do the most wonderful asanas; they break their necks and twist themselves into unbelievable postures. They can do all these body tricks, but some of them are among the angriest people I have ever seen. And then there are mental masters. There are people who are able to move objects through their presence of energy, bending knives and spoons or other things. It does not work that way. You are a prisoner taken hostage by yourself and you are doing all kinds of weird things to justify the takeover. You say "That's okay. I have been hostage for about forty years of life. Another few years to go. I am happy with myself." You have been taken hostage, and the only thing that makes you happy is shock. That is why people love drugs. It shocks the hell out of them when they take drugs. They lose everything. What do they really lose? When people take drugs, there is no catharsis, there is no insight, there is no order, there are no techniques, there is no discipline. However great the shock, it is not real, because people return to their senses and feel more regretful than ever when they realize the reason for their momentary relief. I hope you enjoyed the menu. You are on a cruise ship, and even if you do not like it, that is what will be served. And tipping is not allowed. What I am saying is that this is the time that you can really see a path that will make sense to you. Catharsis and insight engage you with complete obsession for one reason: you engage with each other. Hereafter, do not get caught engaging in catharsis or insight, because they should be gone from your body from tonight. The reason you engaged in these sadomasochistic pleasures with each other or with yourself was because of a restlessness.

There is a restlessness and a nervousness in you because of your inability to make sense out of what is happening, to make sense with reality. If you make sense, not understand, not use catharsis, if you make sense -- which means to feel right about it, you will never be restless. Very simple. The Path of Liberation is the simplest path. That is all I want to say right now. If I tell any more, it will not be about liberation, it will be about discipline. Remember, there is utmost beauty in what you are attempting to get. Never give up. I will not let you, anyway.

Never give up, and hand-in-hand, like a flock of birds -- northbound, southbound, eastbound, and westbound -- all at the same time, you shall ascend. This is the time that the true nature of your life can come to the surface. In the next few weeks and months, you will see more than yourself. In everything that you see there is just yourself, nothing else. There will be a time when you will see more than yourself. That will be the time you will laugh, because there is nothing you can think back on as your own. As long as everything is yours, you can always touch and will be immediately brought back into your past. As a group of birds flies together we will see in many ways how you can really liberate into clear space so that the flight is real and the light is lighter than any light within yourself.

The Path of Liberation is actually breaking the fire that creates the heaviness. However pleasant the warmth is, the fire is burning and killing you. The warmth is very sweet, very comfortable, and you do not know that you are actually burning because it is so pleasurable. Your tail is on fire. You do not feel it because it feels so good. The only way you know it is when you are burnt out, when you are ashes. You have to liberate yourself from the burning fires into the cool breeze. Life is more than great, and it is greater than you.

The Path of Liberation does not mean an enlightenment; it is your qualification to enter into the space of realization. You must be qualified before you can enter into another zone. Remember the Ten Commandments and the Eightfold Noble Path presented by great beings, were introduced to keep people out of trouble. These pathways kept people out of self-sabotage and brought a deep sense of goodness, so that they would mind their own business so to speak, by non-interference and activating mindfulness. These pathways brought people into humble survival and activated their ability to appreciate and to recognize the reverence of living. Traditionally these were neccessary preparations, before breaking the obsession of survival. The path of liberation that was just introduced to you now may ignite a flame of brilliance that can illuminate the world you see as beauty and light. The path of liberation will awaken your energy to total body heat so that there will be no need to recycle your memory and knowledge. There may be a time in the future a man in search of transformation may enter the room and walk gently into the exit sign and come out in hardly any time, but with a profound difference in emotions and body energy. He will be able to see his life, not as a nostalgic memory but rather as a humble appreciation and see his future not as hope and possibilites, but rather as an adventure and an invitation.

The Path of Liberation is a process of revealing, awakening and enlightenment. It lifts you from habitual patterns of seeking pleasure out of nostalgia and sentiment and mental mechanisms of scheming and planning and brings you to a world of clarity and brilliance. When you can see clearly, have a state of no doubt, and are pulsating with passion and energy, the gateways to heavens will automatically open. It is in this life, as who you are, the way you have known, with all the impermanencies and imperfections, that you can find infinite pleasure and joy of living. Life itself, living itself is the pure joy. Life is an infinite experience.

About Tilak

Although it is difficult to describe Tilak and his work, thousands of people around the world, who have met him over the past three decades describe his presence as a gateway that has transformed their lives. Tilak is not a mystic or a guru. His work is not based in any tradition, religion or philosophy. Tilak's presence opens a unique space which allows people to experience a lightness in body and mind.

Born in Sri Lanka in 1943, Tilak as a child dispayed an extraordinary way of making people feel joyful and vibrant by spontaneously creating specific waves of motion and stillness. A fateful accident changed the direction of his life and allowed his full presence to surface in numerous ways that profoundly touched people. From the mid-sixties to seventies, he became reknowned throughout his homeland as a teacher, therapist, friend and guardian to thousands.

Tilak moved to the United States in 1974 at the invitation of several scientists and scholars, making it his permanent residence. Numerous scientific institutes and organizations have been intrigued by Tilak's remarkable abilities.

What Tilak offers is not some startling insight into your own psyche or a cathartic release from emotional pain. Rather it is an opening of a fresh breeze of energy and brilliance which will enable you to live your life without resistance.

Further Information

Numerous talks by Tilak have been recorded and are available in the form of audio and video tapes. These talks have been addressed to live audiences worldwide. For more details on obtaining tapes, attending talks, seminars or special events please contact the following:

Explorations in Consciousness
2183 Sierra Stone Lane
Las Vegas, Nevada 89119
USA

Telephone: 702.260.0444
Fax: 702.260.4828
Internet: breakingreality.org

EBB Publishing
675 Blackhawk Drive
Colorado Springs, Colorado 80919
USA
e-mail: ebbupdate@earthlink.net